PRAISE FOR KINGDOM

"People do not think themselves into a new way of living, but they live themselves into new ways of thinking — a principle strongly and beautifully exemplified here. And Seth Barnes does not stop with new thinking; he leads people to action and engagement where it is needed the most."

—[Fr.] Richard Rohr, O.F.M.

"Seth Barnes captured this great truth about life - that our lives are meant to be fluid and full, a continuum, where every moment, every situation, is part of our ongoing journey to experience God and all that He has for us and through us. Practical, inspiring and full of stories, Kingdom Journeys reveals the joy, risk and adventure of following God, and of allowing that to affect everything about us. A must-read for all ages!

—Brian Heerwagen, CEO, DELTA Ministries International

"Seth Barnes challenges us to engage our greatest question of purpose while experiencing change in our worldview. Only read this book if you care to take a journey that enhances your current story."

—Jeff Shinabarger, Founder, Plywood People

"They say there are no new original thoughts, and while I would not venture an opinion there, I do believe that Seth has captured a new way of at least rethinking about what it means to walk with God in Kingdom Journeys. And oh, how we need fresh thought in this day and age! Thanks, Seth."

—Bill High, President, National Christian Foundation Heartland

"This book is extremely motivating and encouraging to anyone looking to 'be the change they wish to see in the world.' Seth Barnes has a unique ability to inspire and equip both young and old to live out their faith and embrace the Journey God has in store for them."

—Michael Williams, Executive Director, GIANT Impact

"Kingdom Journeys is not just informational but transformational. The life, light and passion of which Barnes speaks of comes with the deliberate understanding we have been created for more than just safe living. Barnes calls us into deep living."

—Tammy Maltby, Author and Speaker

"Two things really set this book apart: first, Seth has something new to say, something important and insightful about faith development (and, particularly, about the faith development of young adults); second, Seth makes reading the book a wonderful adventure with the inclusion of dozens of captivating true stories. Youth workers, pastors, parents, and young adults themselves need to read this book."

—Mark Oestreicher, Partner, The Youth Cartel

"I love it! I've highlighted dozens of passages and if I don't get a grip the whole thing will become a yellow book. I'm usually pretty good at finding fault with other people's idea, but not this time. Kingdom Journeys wraps essential kingdom principles in living stories. I wanted to say it's terrific, but hesitated to use the word because it's cousin to terrifying. Then I realized that's the point. It's terrifying to hate even your own life to follow Christ. It's terrifying to abandon the safety of the familiar, embrace your brokenness, and depend entirely on God. It's terrifying to borrow the discomfort of others and live with it. But that's how disciples are made and why they are rare. In Kingdom Journeys, Seth Barnes confronts the cost of discipleship without losing the sheer adventure of walking with Jesus."

—Daniel Rickett, Author and Executive V.P., She Is Safe

"Jesus said 'Go.' If you have never gone, this book is specifically for you, because Jesus has something of immeasurable value to say to you about you going. If you have already gone, this book is for you, too, because Jesus word to you is still, 'Go.' There is something spiritually catalytic about going. There is something spiritually stagnate about not having gone. Seth Barnes holds a secret for a dynamic spiritual life, and he shares that secret in Kingdom Journeys. God is in the journey he has for you. Don't miss it!"

—Ron Forseth, Vice President, Outreach, Inc., Editor-at-Large, ChurchLeaders.com

"So many comfortable believers I know ask themselves the question, 'How do I really know God is alive? I don't see Him do anything.' When you step out of your comfort zone on a Kingdom Journey, risking all because He said to, the things you experience answer that question. Living on the edge of life and faith is scary. It is not normal for most. A Kingdom Journey takes one out of their comfort zone, away from the easy answers and sharpens ones sensitivity to God's voice. I totally recommend it! Is God calling you to a life of service to the needy on His behalf? Learning to discern His voice and follow His leading is a fundamental part of that calling! And a Kingdom Journey is a valuable 'boot camp' for taking that skill to a new level."

—David Armstrong, Ex. Director, Shorttermmissions.com

"This book is toxic. Toxic. That is, to compromise, complacency and coasting .Not wise to read it if you want to avoid the responsibility or the journey. It has been a joy to walk this journey with Seth for many years now and I can happily confirm that his life is as honest and real as his book. There are literally many thousands of people who bless the day that Seth was born, discovered who he is and who he is Christ and had the guts to set out on this journey not knowing where he was going! I am one of them. Seth is a credit to His Lord, his family and to the Body of Christ. If you hear Christ's call in these pages, He is truly worth following with all your heart."

—Andrew Shearman, Founder and President, G42

"This is an awesome write! If you have been standing on the shore, watching the river go by, afraid to jump in, do not read this book. You will not only jump in the river of journey, but you will get to know who you are as a son/daughter and be on the ride of your life!"

—Gary Black, Founder and President, Rock the Nations

"The walk of faith is a journey in which we seek to meet Jesus at the final destination. Seth Barnes has given us multiple glimpses of meeting Jesus along the way in Kingdom Journeys, as many serve as his hands and feet losing more and more of themselves to gain something far more valuable. His experience, humility, love of the Lord along with practical advice will paint a picture of faith that resonates with many, but I believe in particular to those who know nothing of Christ."

—Kathy Pride, Renegade disciple and author

"If your Christian life seems boring, routine, and stuck in the ordinary, Seth Barnes wants to inject adventure into your journey. In this easy-to-read book, he maps out how.

—Frank Viola, author of *From Eternity to Here and Jesus Manifesto*

"As a parent of two adult children I share Seth's heart to reach and mobilize the next generation. Seth offers the important steps for any parent or leader in raising up a generation of radically-committed disciples. From starting a ministry in his garage to releasing a worldwide movement of over 100,000 missionaries, he shares what it takes to follow Christ in a comfortable world."

—Robert Wolgemuth, Dad, Author, Literary Agent

"Seth Barnes is a ministry innovator of the first order but with his feet firmly planted in the contemplative life. He knows the value of mentoring young people in vital spiritual disciplines all the while promoting the unshakable ethic of service in the tradition of Jesus. And with the heart of a parable framer he knows the power of storytelling. This is a stellar book and one I wish I had read in my twenties."

—Butch Maltby, Consultant

"For far too long, we Christians have only been interested in the destination, when the truth is, without the journey, the destination has little meaning. Seth Barnes understands the power of discovery, and has created a book that will transform your epic journey to becoming the person you were meant to be."

—Phil Cooke, Filmmaker, Speaker, and Author of *One Big Thing: Discovering What You Were Born to Do*

"I am a big proponent of recapturing the classic spiritual disciplines. Seth Barnes has added another key spiritual discipline to my repertoire in his new book, Kingdom Journeys: The Lost Spiritual Discipline. Seth argues convincingly from Scripture, examples from history and his own rich missional experience, that some spiritual growth will never be attained unless we leave it all behind to follow Jesus beyond our comfort zone and status quo. I was convicted, challenged and encouraged as I read this great book. I have another new tool for Kingdom growth: Kingdom Journeys."

—Dr. Ron Walborn, Dean of Alliance Theological Seminary and the College of Bible and Christian Ministry at Nyack College.

"Seth Barnes has done us all a favor by writing a book that desperately needed to be written. While we are drawn to lives of adventure, for some reason inertia can lead to indolence over the course of time and we find ourselves living virtually, from the games we play to the relationships we cultivate. Barnes calls us to get off our couches with his stirring reminder that it takes a physical journey to complete a spiritual one."

—Brian Birdsall, International Representative, Eastern Europe & Russia, Cru.

KINGDOM JOURNEYS:

REDISCOVERING THE LOST SPIRITUAL DISCIPLINE

SETH BARNES

To Mom and Dad,

You lived the journeying life, having met in Yosemite on separate journeys one summer, and then when I came along, packing up for Italy and all points beyond. My Italian may be rusty, but your values still fire in my soul.

You were the first ones to not only believe in me, but believe in the idea that I would never find my purpose in life inside the walls of our home.

Because you took the risk in sending me, I've been freed to pass the favor on to thousands of others. Thanks for the investment of love, hope and tears. It's a debt I can never repay.

I love you guys.

TABLE OF CONTENTS

INTRODUCTION

Hundreds of books talk about our faith walk as a journey, but few delve into the subject of how a physical journey can reinvent and revitalize our spiritual journey with God. If you look at Jesus, you see that he called his disciples to follow him on a physical journey, not just a spiritual one. He tramped around with them in Judea for three years, even sending them out on their own short-term mission trips without him. Everywhere that his team traveled, they talked about the kingdom — a kingdom that wasn't of this world, but was so real. Jesus continually described it for them, comparing it to things they could see like a net, a pearl, and a treasure (in one chapter of the Bible — Matthew 13 — he used no less than seven metaphors to describe the kingdom).

As we explore this subject together, I want to take you alongside some of the people who are on these journeys throughout the world discovering the Kingdom of God. As you hear their stories, let me encourage you to ask the question, "God, do you want me to do something like this? Is this where you're leading me?"

God wants to take you to mountaintops of faith. To do that, he may lead you up the Himalayan Mountains in Nepal, as he did Ruth Wilson, to show you amazing views of his creation. He may call you to abandon your comfortable home, Starbucks, and Sports Center to travel from Florida to Texas on a bicycle, as he did Andrew Maas. He may want you to catch a plane to Swaziland in Africa, like Mallorie Miller did, to help a nation of AIDS victims and experience something of their pain. Or, he may want you to go to inner city Philadelphia, like Claud Crosby, to walk with God through streets lined with drug dealers and addicts.

God teaches through experience, and God may be calling you to experience a kingdom journey, a **real life** journey through the world that will prepare you for your lifelong journey of faith.

CHAPTER 1: MY JOURNEY

"A ship in harbor is safe — but that is not what ships are for."
— John A. Shedd[1]

The road was long and lonely that led from Vienna, Virginia, to Tegucigalpa, Honduras, but my heart was pounding with anticipation as I began to drive. It was the first stage in a kingdom journey that led me to Indonesia, across the world to the Dominican Republic, and back to Virginia.

I ventured out in 1980, right after graduating college. I was all potential and little training. But everything began to change when I set out on my journey. I had gotten my first job—to help start a micro-credit organization in Bali. Training was held in Honduras, so I left Virginia in a yellow Chevy Vega and drove southwest through Texas, crossing the Mexican border at Matamoros. This was the adventure I yearned to live!

The world was full of possibilities. The unknown loomed before me — I relished the feeling of meeting life head-on.

To combat boredom, I picked up eleven hitchhikers along the way. One told me a story about his time in Borneo where he had hunted whales. One evening he was invited to a feast by a tribe of Kalimantan headhunters. They put a plate of mystery meat in front of him and he dug in…

I dropped off my hitchhiking friend in New Orleans and wondered what it would be like to live in a country where head-hunting was still practiced.

After a few days, I arrived — exhausted — in Chiapas, the southernmost state of Mexico. I had been driving without detour or respite, sleeping mostly in my car. I decided to take some time and enjoy the area. I ate dinner in a local restaurant and met an American. He told me about the Mayan ruins and invited me to explore with him. The next day we hiked jungle trails and saw the ruins of Palenque. The heat was intense and we cooled off by sitting beneath the beautifully blue, cascading waterfalls. I couldn't believe how lush and verdant everything was. It was a scene from National Geographic.

As I reflect back on it now, I can see that while it was adventure that got me on the road, there was a price to pay as I went further down it. I didn't know what I didn't know. The world and its pain had barely touched my spirit. My days were organized to meet my personal needs. In time, my priorities would be readjusted, but only as I encountered the painful parts of my kingdom journey.

It took me seven days to get to Honduras; I almost didn't make it. The Vega's engine was barely running on two cylinders by the time I sputtered into Tegucigalpa well after midnight. The first leg of the trip was over.

Two years later, God led me to begin a ministry. Over the next three years, I traveled to Indonesia, flew to Chicago, got married, returned to Indonesia for a year, spent two years in the Caribbean, and then enrolled in business school in Virginia. Since then, I've experienced the vicarious thrill of launching young people into the adventures God prepared for them. Often, they look like variations of my own journeys.

Twenty-seven years later I was back in Chiapas. I was there with a group of fifty twenty-somethings, my own daughter among them. I could see the thrill of adventure in their eyes — a distant echo of what I felt on my own journey.

The morning inched along at Pastor Eleazar's house.

The Mayan jungle steamed around us. That morning the group was preparing to leave on a worldwide journey, one that would take them to thirteen countries, and across four continents to some of the most broken places in the world. They were embarking on a missions adventure called the World Race. And while the first leg of their journey was just beginning there in Chiapas, for me, this was a return. These young visionaries would see the world like never before; volunteering with churches, orphanages, and other ministries. Along the way, God would use them to help *me* rediscover pilgrimage, a lost spiritual discipline.

That morning I got my coffee, read e-mails, and chatted with a few people about their upcoming journey. After a few hours, it was time for church. We piled into vans and drove through the jungle, passing the turnoff to the Mayan ruins where *Apocalypto* was filmed. We followed the twisting road through *Zapatista* guerrilla territory and drove up the mountains to the small village of Arroyo Palenque where the team would worship before their launch.

The villagers stared as we got out of the vans, a huge posse of gringos. We packed the church to the rafters, standing side-by-side with our native hosts. As we waited, a tangible expectation hung in the humid air. Someone began to sing. The song was picked up by the villagers and then, slowly, by us. The concrete walls started to pulsate with the sounds of praises to God being sung in English, Spanish, and Ch'ol.

As we worshiped, memories of my own journey flooded my thoughts. God was reminding me of my own journey. I remembered with chills God's promise to me twenty-seven years before. "You'll be back," I had sensed him saying. "There's something here for you." In college, the Lord convicted me to "loose the chains of injustice," and I committed my life to helping others understand that they can make a difference. Looking back, I see that I didn't yet understand the baggage weighing me down or the unhealed wounds that I hid. I wanted to fully respond to God's call, but my faith was shallower than I realized. I had trusted Jesus to save me from hell, but I hadn't begun to understand the life he offered *before* death. The stories in the Bible about the disciples being forced to trust him completely didn't yet make sense to me.

As we worshiped in the church in Mexico, God turned my thoughts back to that first journey through Chiapas. He showed me in a fresh way how it was part of a larger pilgrimage, a life-long journey that I am still on; a journey that I will always be on.

The music stopped. The villagers stared as the pastor handed me the microphone. He wanted me to preach? I had nothing prepared except the thoughts about this journey God had me on and maybe about how we all need a journey.

So that's where I started — I began to tell my story about the last time I had driven by their village, about my week-long trip to Honduras that led me through Palenque, how the extraordinary journey circled back on itself and landed

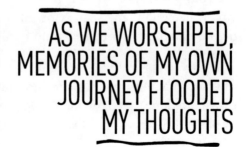

AS WE WORSHIPED, MEMORIES OF MY OWN JOURNEY FLOODED MY THOUGHTS

me in their church. I told them that if I hadn't abandoned the comforts of home, I would not have experienced the challenges that enabled me to discover new truths about God, his world, and myself. Without the journey, the road trip to Honduras, life in the island capitals of Jakarta and Santo Domingo…without the physical adversity and pain of a physical journey, I would have missed important lessons along the way.

I will always think of Chiapas as the place where my journeys collided. *It took a physical journey to complete a spiritual one.*

The church service ended. We hugged our new friends goodbye, returned to our vans, and drove back to Pastor Eleazar's house. The teams were eager to get going. Before long, they left to spend a year traveling around the world. I headed back to my wife and kids — on another leg in my kingdom journey.

WHAT IS A KINGDOM JOURNEY?

I went jogging before leaving Mexico. Near our home base was a wide-open field that stretched miles in every direction — a great place for a run. It's also the local trash dump. All of the city's garbage is piled into a huge mountain in the middle of the field. I ran a mile across the field to the trash heap and bore left. I was in the zone. My only thoughts were about the young leaders who were taking the first of what I hoped would become many such trips. At that point, I only had a dream of what *this* journey could become.

Wrapped up in these thoughts, I wasn't paying attention as I ran. When it came time to head home, I turned around, disoriented, not recognizing the landscape and with a pang of panic, I realized I was lost!

Not knowing what to do, I kept running, following goat paths past cacti and sagebrush. I ran without bearings past scattered trash — the filth of the city. I ran for miles and miles — praying one of those "oh-God-get-me-out-of-this-one" prayers all the while.

After a while, I sensed God saying, "Go back to the trash heap and start over." Like most runners, I hated to backtrack, but I listened. I headed to the mountain of trash in the center of the field. A sense of peace slowly returned. Then I recognized a dirt road in the distance. I took it and found that I was heading home. What began as a run grew into a mini-pilgrimage. "Whenever you get lost," God seemed to say, "look for me at the trash heap. I'll show you the way home."

So often, we get lost in self-absorbed thinking. We look for Jesus in Bible studies and self-help books, and he doesn't seem to be around. *We need to look for him near the trash heap.* If we live in suburbia, we may need to take a journey to get there. Every time I've looked for Christ in a slum or a dump, I have found him. He is reflected in the eyes of a dirty child. He waves to me through an old woman with wrinkles engraved in her cheeks. "Blessed are the poor in spirit," (Matthew 5:3) he says. Perhaps his point is they are blessed because he makes his home with them. We sometimes get lost in this modern world, far from Jesus and ourselves. God gave us this concept of sacred, intentional travel as a means of finding our way back.

MORE THAN A PILGRIMAGE

Generations ago, we had the concept of *pilgrimage* — something that may have felt like an intense spiritual discipline. It was a journey to discover where God lives in the world. It was a discipline founded by Jesus himself.

"Go," Christ says to his disciples, "I am sending you out like lambs amongst wolves. Do not take a purse or bag or sandals. When you enter a town…heal the sick who are there and tell them, 'The kingdom of God is near you'" (Luke 10:3-4). The Bible shows Jesus instituting this type of pilgrimage in Luke 9 and 10; Matthew 10, and Mark 6. Jesus sent his disciples out to discover the kingdom with absolutely no provisions. Their mission: to show and tell those they met about what they had found.

When people go on a pilgrimage to a holy shrine, they go to discover God. But in so doing, they find that God is not in the destination, but the journey. When I went on my run, I found God in the trash heap. I carried him back with me. Everything after that somehow seemed holier. A kingdom journey removes the scales from our eyes and allows us to see God all around and even within.

We see different societies around the world introducing their young people to spiritual reality through the process of a journey. In some Native American tribes, a young man goes into the wild with nothing — no food, no drink, and no weapons. He leaves and stays gone until he is starved, dehydrated, and possibly delusional.

At some point, God or something buried deep inside of the man manifests. The experience is thought to connect him to nature, himself, and to the spiritual world. It is more than a boy learning how to be a man. It is a life lesson, teaching him that he is connected to a deeper reality. This deeper reality is what Jesus called the "kingdom."

JOURNEYS OPEN UP POSSIBILITIES

Journeys open up our spirit to the possibility of a reality it hasn't yet grasped. Away from the familiar, our hearts become a place where God can work, a place where only faith will sustain us. Even though our physical travels may not last a year, the lessons we learn will continue to rend our hearts for years to come. The journey is more than an escape from the things that have come to define us in life — it's a chance to break free from the shackles of an ordinary existence.

A kingdom journey opens up your identity for you to examine. Identity is much easier to tear down than define. Back home, *you* are the frustration you feel when you're not getting treated the way you deserve. You may see yourself under pressure, experiencing road rage and wonder, "Who am I becoming?" On your journey, the reverse is true — you are the compassion you feel when you hold a little girl orphaned by AIDS. You are the anger mixed with hurt towards a glue-sniffing street boy who stole your camera.

Moments like these lead to a place where you begin to understand what Jesus meant when he said to pick up your cross — that instrument of death to self — daily. This is painful, but necessary. Yes, these transient reactions to your experience are only *you in the moment,* a snapshot. Stack them end-to-end and they are points on a line that lead to a new sense of identity.

Somewhere in the midst of our journeying, we begin to wake up to spiritual reality. What was blurry, starts to come into focus. And when it does, we can't help but ask, "Why? Why does a journey do this? Why do I have to leave when all I need is already around me?"

JESUS AND JOURNEY

A journey is an act of leaving — a process of physical abandon that teaches us how to do the same spiritually. Perhaps, to find your true identity you need to abandon everything else.

We know what Jesus said about the journey to which he invited his disciples on:

- To discover the kingdom, you have to lay aside your possessions and go on the road with him (Mark 10:17-27).

- To find your calling, you have to quit your job. "Leave your nets," he says to us. "Follow me...and I will make you fishers of men" (Mark 1:17-18).

- To see the dead raised, you have to leave the funeral. "Follow me," he commands. "Let the dead bury their own dead" (Luke 9:60).

- To become rich, you have to give up everything. If you want to be perfect, go, "sell your possessions and give to the poor." You will have "treasure in heaven." Then come, follow me (Luke 12:33).

- To get what you want, you have to abandon desire. "Whoever wants to be my disciple must deny himself and take up their cross daily and follow me" (Luke 9:23).

We go on a journey because he tells us to go - to leave. In physically leaving, we discover spiritual possibilities. Jesus spent three years leaving places, leaving people before finally leaving life itself. To know Jesus, you have to learn how to leave. In the end, the leaving is the finding. You abandon your earthly treasure; you receive a treasure in heaven. You abandon your father and your mother; you get the family of God. You abandon your life, and like a seed that dies and grows a hundred times its size, you find new abundant life.

WHY GO ON A KINGDOM JOURNEY?

All of us are on a journey. We can't escape the beginning and the end, but the middle is full of crazy possibilities. Distractions attempt to dumb us down and make our journey comfortable. Our society tries to level out the scary parts of what can feel like a roller coaster ride. Is it any wonder that the default for most people is to make the journey easy? Better to park the car in the driveway, punch your ticket at a secure job for forty years, and then retire somewhere before they ship you off to a nursing home. *Or not.*

A few questions may help you along the way

- Where is your life headed?

- What is the purpose for your existence?

- When will you really be satisfied?

Examining your motives can help you understand if you're selling out to the status quo. Are you organizing your life around a career track? Does the smallness of your vision for life risk landing you in a scene from television's *The Office*?

I pray that you're not already there — feeling boxed in by routine, bored by the daily grind, unable to see your way out of it, and wondering if you're living the best version of your life.

Perhaps even now, something inside of you is longing for a pilgrimage — a plunging into mystery and possibility; a glimpse of who you could become if only you weren't saddled by so many expectations.

Maybe it's time you let God send you on a journey. He wants to take you on an adventure to experience the most amazing things in the world.

Wherever you go, I believe you'll discover that he'll meet you on the way in a variety of disguises and at the most unexpected moments. When he does, it will cause you to put your status-quo self into foreclosure and put a down payment on your truest self. And, like so many before you, you will look back to celebrate that day you began to live as your true self, the day you chose to leave.

So here's my invitation: How about it?

Let's journey together.

CHAPTER 1 NOTES

1. John A. Shedd, "Salt from my Attic," in *The Yale Book of Quotations 2006,*ed. Fred R. Shapiro (New Haven, CT: Yale University Press, 2006), 705.

CHAPTER 1: THE GIFT OF RESTLESSNESS

"I am always doing that which I cannot do, in order that I may learn how to do it." — Pablo Picasso[2]

While we are all on a journey through life, it takes a kingdom journey to make us into the man or woman God wants us to be. It might start out as nothing but the urge to escape. We might feel claustrophobic, trapped, and just want out. Remember how middle school felt? That's what I'm talking about.

As a seventh grader, I remember the terror of P.E. class. Weighing all of seventy-seven pounds, I found myself (through what must have been an administrative error or a mean joke) in the same class as the entire ninth-grade football team. Most of these guys were twice my size. Dodge ball is a horrifying exercise in humiliation: a violent assault of red rubber balls thrown by your opponents. I was an easy target. The only thing my memory hasn't successfully repressed is my feeble attempt to hide behind the bleachers.

It didn't work.

My middle school years were a cruel phase of life. It's a chapter I'd rather skip over. Wouldn't you? What a way to start kids toward a healthy, successful, and well-balanced adulthood!

Thankfully, when I was in high school, my mother had a vision for me to go on a mission trip. I couldn't have cared less about the "mission", but I wanted to please her. So, I signed up and was forced to find financial supporters and prayer partners. Full of trepidation, I accompanied my mom on visits to her friends to ask for prayer. I had no clue what to say. I didn't feel nearly spiritual enough to go. Frankly, if there was anything that attracted me to the trip it was the idea of seeing the world.

The mission agency brochure described the local markets where I could buy colorful handicrafts. The beautiful green volcanoes surrounding Lake Atitlan sounded enchanting. As a teenager from the Midwest, I knew little of such wonders. I had neither the imagination nor the vocabulary to understand the world of ministry, but I could hear the world of travel and the mystery of foreign cultures calling my name.

Full of mixed motives, I began the trip that would change my life. God began to take me from selfishness to compassion. Yes, the volcanoes were spectacular and the Mayan markets were exotic, but along the way God exposed my heart to people he loved. The adventure began a work in me that I could not do for myself, certainly not in my hometown.

It was much more than the taste for adventure that caused me to go to Guatemala. It was restlessness — a stirring in my spirit that I couldn't shake. Columbia, Missouri, was too small for the dreams that hadn't even begun to crystallize in my spirit, but that I sensed were coming. So I had to get going — I had to leave. I'd been overseas. What I'd seen had whispered, "There's more," though I could only guess at what "more" might be.

The urge to leave was unsettling. I've found that most people experience it at some point in their life. Claud Crosby and Jessi Marquez are great examples. I first met eighteen-year-old Claud at our ministry base in Philadelphia. I connected with Jessi a decade later. Both came to me on the front edge of the journeys that would change their lives.

Prior to moving to Pennsylvania, Claud rode his BMX bike six to eight hours a day. He played the drums for several bands. He listened to hardcore music that combined thrashing guitars and political extremism. He studied just enough to get by. In 2000, he declared to his father that he wasn't going to college. "We'll see about that," his dad replied. In a few months, Claud was enrolled in a South Carolina college studying sculpture and photography.

I asked Claud if he studied art because he wanted to be an artist. "No, but I had to study something," he told me. He transferred from one college to another, three different schools in two years. His disdain for formal education outlasted his father's efforts to keep him in school. Finally, he dropped out altogether two weeks into his junior year. His father was not pleased.

Jean Twenge, a psychology professor at San Diego State University, says people like Claud are products of a school system that taught three-year-olds to sing, "I'm special/I'm special/ Look at me."[3] Youth tee-ball leagues give every kid a trophy. Parents file lawsuits if their kids got hurt. "By cushioning feeling *bad*," says Dr. Archibald Hart, a psychologist and professor at Fuller Seminary, "the self-esteem movement has made it harder for us to feel *good*. It has encouraged cheap success."[4] The generation of young people now entering their twenties, Twenge says, feels entitled to success. Their expectations are based in fantasy, not reality. According to Twenge, "More and more young people are going to find themselves at thirty without a viable career, a house, or any semblance of stability."[5]

This seems to be where Claud's life was headed. He was a college dropout who found himself attracted to extreme subcultures. It's easy to imagine how his life could have worked out — perhaps at a call center or as a night security guard to pay the bills so he could go clubbing on the weekends. But something happened to Claud that changed the course of his life.

By 2011, Claud was married to a hearing-impaired woman and had adopted two daughters from the AIDS-ravaged nation of Swaziland. A medical researcher by day, Claud pursues his bachelor's degree in pre-med at night. He plans to attend medical school in Lebanon or Pakistan. After that, he hopes to practice medicine in the Congo. Claud changed from an adolescent who, according to some experts, was on the road to social instability to a man with purpose, focus, and responsibility. What caused such a dramatic shift?

It all began when he made the decision to listen to the whisper inside that said, "leave."

WHAT DO THE EXPERTS SAY?

Jessi Marquez could relate to the clubbing phase of Claud's life. Living in Manhattan and working as an event planner for New York City's rich and famous, Jessi was the life of the party. She earned a good salary, but was unable to pay her rent because of her affection towards buying Louis Vuitton duffels, $1,000 heels, and Lily Pulitzer dresses. The glitz didn't satisfy.

"When it came down to it, I hated myself," she recalled. "I was going out seven nights a week because the thought of being alone seemed like torture. I was exhausted, filled with anxiety, and teetering on depression."

Around the time Jessi was born, her mother began her own Kingdom Journey. She became a born again Christian, promising God to choose a new life for the both of them. Wanting nothing to do with Christianity, Jessi's father left. He just disappeared, never to be found.

That trauma of abandonment made her afraid of rejection and caused her to do anything to get others' approval. She became a chameleon. If she partied on the Upper East Side, she would dress the "prepster" part. If she was on the Lower East Side, she made herself into a "hipster."

Jessi never questioned the reality of God. Growing up in a Christian home, she had plenty of opportunities to learn about God. She just didn't see the point. When she had a problem, her mom told her to pray about it. "But Mom, I don't get it," she would say. "How is praying going to pay my rent? How is praying going to soften the pain in my heart?"

The pattern of Jessi's life looked great on the outside. But on the inside, she was withering. Depressed, lonely, and insecure, she knew something had to change. Her way of life wasn't sustainable.

In the space of a year, Jessi's life was turned upside down. She went from a hollow meaningless existence to helping plant churches in Manhattan. She quit her job and started a non-profit. A natural networker and salesperson, she used her innate skills to attract dozens of people to church.

She stopped being influenced by the nightlife lifestyle. Instead, she became the influence. She was no longer ruled by an intense fear of rejection. What caused the change that turned Jessi's life around spiritually?

It started with an unsettledness that wouldn't go away until she left it all.

THE URGE

In the late eighteenth century, hundreds of men set out to explore the most desolate spots on earth: the Arctic poles. These adventurers were considered heroes. Many died. Those who survived — by sheer strength of will, instinct, or dumb luck — carved out a place in history for themselves. When I ponder their pain and endurance, I can't help but be challenged and inspired. What compelled these men to throw themselves into the rawness of nature?

An advertisement placed by Ernest Shackleton appealed to the universal human urge to explore the unknown. "Men wanted for hazardous journey. Small wages, bitter cold, long months of complete darkness, constant danger, and safe return doubtful. Honor and recognition in case of success." Men volunteered by the hundreds.[6] What were they seeking? Perhaps these were heroes searching for God.

They sought him in the crystal crags and frozen tundra — even in themselves and their will to survive.

We are all compelled by a yearning for eternity — by the possibility of the divine. St. Augustine of Hippo wrote "Lord...you have made us for yourself, and our heart is restless until it rests in you."[7] When we talk about living with a "God-shaped hole," it is this longing for God that is born within each of us. We are intrigued by its allure and mystery. What would you risk for a glimpse of God? Would you trudge thousands of miles until your toes froze?

A GENERATION FULLY ALIVE

For too long, a generation has been coddled, distracted, and under-challenged. The generation — too often like Claud did — throw themselves into sports and video games. They are a generation of Jessis, emotionally shape-shifting to please their friends, while inside feeling lonely and hopeless. This is the most educated group of young adults in the history of the world, yet they value their education less than any other. Many are born into economic privilege and squander it on credit card debt. They are numb, asleep to the realities of the world. So, my question is: "How do we wake them up?"

First, let's agree on what not to do. We don't need to educate them further. For more than 400 years the church's primary method of discipleship has been teaching. In 1637 Descartes said, "I think; hence, I am."[8] Ever since, the Western world has held onto reason as its highest virtue.

Our culture says, "If you can't measure it, it doesn't exist." According to the Barna Group, as of 2010, Millennials — the generation born between 1980 and 1995 — are twice as likely as their parents to quit church and check out on their faith.[9] What will turn this trend around? What will wake them up? I suggest that they need a journey.

A few years ago, I was standing on the shores of Lake Nicaragua. In the distance was the volcano on Ometepe Island. It was 5:45 a.m. and the first glint of dawn illuminated the landscape. Suddenly, the serenity of the moment was shattered as a huge flock of swallows swooped down the sand dunes, almost brushing my ankles. They skimmed the ground and flew over the lake like miniature stealth fighter jets in formation. They were heading toward Ometepe Island.

Breathtaking. Maybe a million birds rushed into ferocious

headwinds over a stretch of shore perhaps a mile long. They kept coming for almost ten minutes. Each day I was in Nicaragua, I stood by the lake. Each morning the birds showed up, buzzing by my ankles. They never reached the island. Perhaps there was an insect swarm way out on the lake. Perhaps it was avian "morning calisthenics." I don't know. Whatever it was, the swallows were a great illustration of a dream to which I've dedicated my life.

In my dream I see a generation of young people abandon their comfortable lives to fly in great numbers out into the harsh world to cover it with the glory of God. Their quest will seem reckless to those committed to a life of self-interest. They will appear impetuous to those measuring their commitment to follow Jesus according to careful risk-versus-reward formulas. They must go. The world is waiting for them.

THE SPIRITUAL DISCIPLINES

Understanding that almost any behavioral change is rooted in personal transformation, I've looked at spiritual disciplines as I've tried to realize this dream. Most of us are good at asking, "How do we change on the inside? How do we become more loving, selfless, and forgiving?" But merely willing yourself to change doesn't work. Behavioral changes result from deep inner change. What people see on the outside is the result of what's happening on the inside.

The religious people of Jesus' day were criticized for working hard to do good things on the outside while on the inside they were dead. "White-washed tombs," Jesus called them. Maybe you can relate.

Richard Foster wrote the classic book, *The Celebration of Discipline.*[10] It's still relevant after more than thirty years. Why?

Because it deals with how we change the inside. His answer to that question is curious. Foster makes the case that inward change happens by doing things on the outside: activities like prayer, meditation, fasting, worship, and confession. Such practices give God time and space to change us and help us become better versions of ourselves. Foster warns that it's not by works that we are saved, but when we change the exterior, we give God access to transform the interior. He cites twelve specific disciplines:

• Study	• Solitude	• Confession
• Prayer	• Service	• Worship
• Fasting	• Simplicity	• Guidance
• Meditation	• Submission	• Celebration

Spiritual disciplines are essential to becoming more alive in Christ. Can you imagine trying to become closer to God without prayer? Yet, Foster's list has its drawbacks. Have you ever tried to adopt one (or several) of these disciplines? Maybe you began reading your Bible each morning or tried to pray at a certain time every day. Maybe you tried volunteering with a ministry or at a homeless shelter. How long did it last?

Most of us start strong. We wake up with enthusiasm. When we sit down to pray, we feel refreshed and excited to connect with the Lord. When we show up at the homeless shelter, we can't wait to help.

Then, it becomes harder. Perhaps we miss a day of Bible study because we sleep through our alarm. We're bored during prayer time and get distracted. Our discipline of service flags when the homeless don't really want to talk to us. Our enthusiasm may sustain for us for a while. We think, "I just need to recommit and focus. I can do it if I just try harder."

Then, we sleep through Bible study three days in a row. We have to do our laundry and don't have time to pray. We decide we'd rather go to the beach with our friends than to the homeless shelter. Having failed to summon the necessary discipline, we chastise ourselves. We feel guilty, but we can't get back into our routine. Our regimen has become another failed New Year's resolution.

Even when we follow through with spiritual disciplines, the results can be spotty. They're kind of like brushing our teeth. They provide good hygiene, but if we want to get our teeth really white, we have to go on some kind of program, usually one recommended by a professional. So how do we change if we can't even stick to the disciplines that are supposed revitalize us? We need something else to help motivate us to follow a spiritual discipline.

For years, I have looked for something that would turbo-charge a person's faith walk in a way that doesn't depend so heavily on will power.

Finally, I found one. The answer came from Jesus himself. It's a practice he instituted with his disciples, one that bore tremendous results. A discipline we've neglected: a kingdom journey.

CHAPTER 2 NOTES

2. Pablo Picasso, Thinkexist.com, http://thinkexist. com/quotation/i_am_always_doing_that_which_i_ cannot_do-in_order/217965.html.

3. Jean Twenge and W. Keith Campbell, *The Narcissism Epidemic: Living in the Age of Entitlement* (New York: Free Press, 2009), 16.

4. Kelly Monroe Kullberg and Lael Arrington, *A Faith and Culture Devotional: Daily Readings in Art, Science, and Life*, (Grand Rapids, MI: Zondervan, 2008), 148.

5. Twenge and Campbell, *The Narcissism Epidemic*, 83.

6. Wikipedia, http://en.wikipedia.org/wiki/ Endurance_%281912_ship%29.

7. St. Augustine, *Confessions*, trans. Henry Chadwick (Oxford, England: Oxford University Press, 2008), 3.

8. René Descartes, *A Discourse on Method: Meditations on the First Philosophy Principles of Philosophy*, trans. John Veitch (London, England: Orion Publishing Group, 2004), 26.

9. Pew Forum on Religion and Public Life, "Religion Among the Millennials," http://www.pewforum.org/Age/ Religion-Among-the-Millennials.aspx.

10. Richard J. Foster, *Celebration of Discipline*, (New York: HarperCollins Publishers Inc., 1998), listed first in contents.

CHAPTER 3: HOW DID JESUS DO IT?

"Without faith it is impossible to please God." — Hebrews 11:6

When I began pondering what it might take to help awaken a generation, I studied how Jesus discipled his followers — how he raised them up into maturity. And I discovered a detail about the way Jesus discipled that transformed the way I now approach discipleship. That truth also changed the lives of people like Claud and Jessi.

Consider Jesus' mindset. His purpose wasn't modest. He wanted to save the whole world.

Imagine yourself starting a movement — a worldwide explosion of transformed people — who would then turn the world upside down. How would *you* do it? To reach as many people as possible, you might go to the local stadium, rent it out for the weekend, and put up flyers all over the city. You might hope and pray for huge crowds to pack the venue.

Of course, Jesus didn't do it that way. He spoke to huge crowds a few times, but mostly he avoided them. What did he do? He sought quiet places and hung out with a small group of followers. Sometimes, he even told people not to tell anyone about him. He was the perfect example of how *not* to market a new movement.

I once asked Dr. Peter Lord, a prolific author and teacher who has spoken to hundreds of thousands during his ministry, what he would have done differently. He was in his seventies at the time and was reflecting on a life dedicated to Christ. His insight surprised me.

"I wouldn't have preached so much," Dr. Lord said with a sigh. "No one remembers what you say, anyway." He said he wouldn't have had a church larger than twelve people. He explained, "Once you get bigger than that, the weak people don't speak up." He paused, looked at me intently, and said, "Church is *for* the weak." Though it was years ago, the stunning simplicity of that truth refreshes me even today.

How did Jesus start a movement? He chose twelve men and asked them to follow him, live with him, and learn to do life as he did. Jesus wanted them to learn to imitate him. That's what Peter did when he left the safety of a boat in the middle of a storm to walk on water. He saw Jesus do it and Peter was bold enough to try, too.

Paul echoed this idea to the people of Corinth when he said, "I urge you to imitate me." He said he was sending Timothy, who would "remind you of my way of life in Christ Jesus." Apparently, Timothy had been imitating Paul for so long that he was a living example of him. *Paul imitates Jesus. Timothy imitates Paul. The Corinthians were to imitate Timothy.* This is how it works.

God doesn't ask us to innovate, but to imitate. Creativity and spontaneity are prized, but what we really need are people bold enough to follow in the footsteps of our spiritual predecessors. They say imitation is the sincerest form of flattery. It is also the most effective means of disciple-making. Gordon MacDonald summarizes this well:

> "Mature Christians don't grow through programs or through the mesmerizing delivery of a talented speaker or worship band. Would-be saints are mentored — one-on-one or, better yet, one-on-small group (three to twelve was Jesus' model). Mature Christians are made one-by-one through the influence of other Christians already mature."[11]

Gradually, my eyes began to open. I began to look at my faith in a whole new way. Had I had found the answer to my discipleship quest? If I understood correctly, disciples are not born, they are developed — through a holy partnership between God and the teachers he provides.

When looking around for examples, I was disappointed at how far many contemporary well-intended ministries seemed to have moved from this model. Where was the discipleship I read about in the Scriptures? Where were the Pauls and the Timothys asking others to imitate them as they imitated Christ? Where was the movement that was supposed to turn the world upside down?

THE STATE OF AFFAIRS IN AMERICA

When I was in high school, a youth worker took me out for a milkshake. I had never met him before and I thought, "Why did this older guy single me out?" I was mystified, but also flattered. I don't remember what we talked about, other

GOD DOESN'T ASK US TO INNOVATE, BUT TO IMITATE.

than him communicating to me that I mattered through that simple act and by sharing an hour of his life.

During my teenage years I lived in a dark room of exile. For a brief moment, a door was opened, and light flooded in. Then it slammed shut again. That meeting was the only one-on-one he and I ever had. I don't remember his name and I'm sure he's forgotten mine. Other than my parents' efforts, that was the sum total of my one-on-one discipleship. Kind of pitiful, but what's worse, it's more than many people get.

Can you relate? As I talk to people, my milkshake experience seems to typify the state of disciple-making in America today. It raises the question, "Why do we struggle so much with this thing called discipleship?"

How hard is a weekly conversation at a coffee shop? I don't say this to be critical, but attempts at discipleship — as with nurturing a houseplant or a goldfish — die from lack of consistent attention. Maybe it's our busyness or concern for efficiency. Whatever it is, we need a change. One thing my negative personal experiences taught me was I realized there's no replacing relational connection to help people grow spiritually. If we are to awaken a generation, discipleship is key.

So, I had this dream and knew that if I was to start working on it, I needed to understand how to make disciples. I lacked experience. Not knowing where else to begin, I experimented.

EXPERIMENTS IN DISCIPLESHIP

I'm a born risk-taker, a ministry entrepreneur. I love to look for new ways of giving life to people. Most of the time my experiments fail. Sometimes, they blow up as they launch, but every once in a while, I witness God breathe life into a new project.

I've experimented with all sorts of approaches to discipleship. I started a blog, thinking the people I'm discipling could read it every day and interact with me through comments and e-mail. Through it, I've connected with thousands of people, young and old, from all over the world. I've met face-to-face with some of them regularly. A few have begun long-term discipleship relationships themselves. My relationship with Gabe Landes is a good example.

Gabe began as a blog reader and then became more of a participant in the blog community. He introduced his wife, Heidi, to the community. They eventually led small groups and mission trips with their virtual disciples. Since then, we've dreamed together about planting the kingdom of God around the world.

Here is some of the fruit:

- Together, we have supported orphans and disaster relief in Pakistan

- We've led online studies on listening prayer

- We have organized a leadership retreat

- We have gone on vision trips in Africa

- We are starting to plant churches

Our relationship shows that while technology is valuable,

it is a poor substitute for actual human contact. To go deep with people, you need to physically be with them. It's the difference between staring at a computer screen and sharing a milkshake with someone.

LESSONS FROM PERU

In 2002 I attempted another discipleship experiment. Recognizing that my teenage children needed to see and experience the supernatural, I took them and seventeen others to Peru on a month-long mission trip. For much of the year leading up to the project, we studied the book of Acts. Once we were in Peru, we put it into practice worshiping and praying each day before traveling out to the slums nearby. We planted five churches.

One day, my son, Seth Jr., inspired by having read about the power of God in the book of Acts, prayed for a bed-ridden man to walk. After praying, he told the man, "I want you to prove you've been healed. Get up and walk around!" Then he watched in amazement as the man stood up, put his shoes on, and walked into the sunshine outside! As Seth recalled, "The man was so excited, he bent down to touch his toes like fifty times and picked up his granddaughter and kissed her!"

Talia, my daughter, met Secundina, a woman who had pancreatic cancer. Every day she returned to Secundina's house, praying with her and ultimately helping plant a home church in her living room. Unlike Seth, Talia didn't see an immediate answer to her prayers, but several years later, she was able to return and visit Secundina. Talia was thrilled to see that she had been healed — she was cancer-free!

One participant, Eugene, had his life changed in a way none of us expected. One night, I sensed that God had a word for him. I passed it on to him, "Go to China." After returning home, that's exactly what he did. He left for China later that year on a scouting trip. Eugene subsequently dropped out of college, left everything, and returned to China. He's still there today with a team of disciples.

Another participant, Miguel, moved to the Dominican Republic and is devoting his life to raising Dominican disciples who would then make disciples around the Caribbean. He dreams of planting churches in Cuba.

Even my two female co-leaders on that trip had their lives changed. They often return to Peru and other parts of South America. They lead their own trips now, following up on the churches we planted during that one brief month. One of the churches we planted sends out its own missionaries high into the Andes Mountains. A recent mission team met them there and was amazed to see this group of disciples imitating what they saw in us. They were reaching people in remote areas. Who knows where God may send those new believers?

THE BIG DISCOVERY

Literature, it could be argued, is marked by two main urges. The first urge is the quest for significance: to make your place in the world, to be someone. Think of the American Dream, the belief that if you work hard enough you can become someone great. The second urge is the opposite: to leave it all for the open road. Escape and adventure.

Think of the heroic epics: Perseus leaves home on a perilous voyage, John Wayne rides off into the sunset, and Luke Skywalker flies out into the universe. It's something far more significant than restlessness. Books, magazines, music, and art are saturated with it — this innate desire to seek out strange new worlds and live an adventure.

"There's a feeling I get when I look to the west/and my spirit is crying for leaving," sang Led Zeppelin.[12]

"Tramps like us, baby we were born to run," sings Springsteen.[13]

"I think I'll go to Boston/I think I'll start a new life/I think I'll start it over, where no one knows my name," says Augustana.[14]

When we follow our instincts to travel, we search for something deeply spiritual. It was obvious with the polar explorers, less so with the Beat generation. The Beat generation believed they could hit their own mother lode of purpose and insight in the deserts and highways out West. Men like Kerouac gave us glimpses of the story: "It was a wild yea-saying burst of American joy; it was Western, the west wind, an ode from the Plains, something new, long prophesied, long a-coming."[15] There was something out there, they thought, something they needed to find. Their restlessness drove them to the open road.

The hippies of the 1960s and 1970s repeated the urge like a chorus. Joni Mitchell's "Rainy Night House" ends:

"So you packed your tent and went
To live out in the Arizona sand
You are a refugee
From a wealthy family
You gave up all the golden factories
To see, who in the world you might be."[16]

Young people fled cities and set up communes in forests and deserts. They looked to settle in the loneliest nooks and crannies of the country. Disillusioned with the "establishment," they wore hand-woven clothes and grew their own food. They were looking for something they couldn't find in the city.

Restlessness is an itch that, if left unscratched, is a curse. The Curse of Restlessness is everywhere. It may even be in you. If you have felt it, you know what I mean. It seizes you in a way that makes you believe nothing but leaving is good enough. That everything around you is empty, superficial and too complicated. You sense that the sacred life — something you've only experienced in scattered moments — is somewhere out *there*. You *must* go find it.

Restlessness can be one of the most frustrating human emotions. It whispers: "I hate it here. Anywhere would be better than *this*." It makes us want to take impetuous leaps into the unknown. It causes us to create elaborate fantasies: El Dorado, the City of Gold, or whatever Kerouac and others longed for when they hit the road.

The Curse of Restlessness can cause us to escape in unhealthy ways. Idealizing the past, we may fall into the cliché of recalling our "glory days," whether they were during high school, college, or those years before getting married. We think, "If I could just go back, if I could do it again. With everything I've learned I could do it right this time." Solomon says, "A fool's eyes wander to the ends of the earth," (Proverbs 17:24). If we allow the Curse to speak to us like that, it will pollute every part of our lives.

WE YEARN FOR SOMETHING MORE, A HARDWIRING TO SEARCH FOR THE KINGDOM OF GOD ITSELF.

Why does restlessness plague us? Maybe it's an echo of Eden — an ancient glimmer of what paradise must be like. We yearn for something more, a hardwiring to search for the kingdom of God itself. That's why, for all of its consequences and pitfalls, restlessness is not a curse. Restlessness is a gift.

I've been discipling young people for a while now. As we get into some of the deeper hidden things in their lives, restlessness almost invariably comes up. Again and again, I've had young people tell me they just want to leave. They are tired of their routine lives, dead-end jobs, and never-ending schoolwork. They want an escape. Restlessness is commonly manifested in hobbies or addictions. Individuals fantasize about leaving everything without telling anyone, maybe to hitchhike across America, or travel the world. They rarely do it, but this urge is deep in their subconscious.

After talking to hundreds of men and women, I've developed a theory: In every generation, humans have felt the Curse — and Gift — of Restlessness. I believe Abraham had it. Gandhi had it. George Washington had it.

At some point, we all just want to leave.

TAKE NO SHOES

Traditional peoples found ways to turn the Curse of Restlessness into the Gift of Restlessness by weaving it into the sacred. They made a spiritual discipline out of leaving. Some call it a pilgrimage or a rite of passage or an initiation experience. In Australia it's known as a "walkabout." The essence has always been about tapping into restlessness to help people to discover the divine at work: both in the world and in themselves. Their journey turned The Curse into the Gift it was meant to be.

Jesus did this, too. He tapped into his would-be disciples'

itch to leave by calling them with a holy challenge, "Foxes have dens and birds have nests, but the Son of Man has no place to lay his head…Follow me" (Luke 9:58-59). Many did follow. Jesus transformed the Curse of Restlessness into a calling that enabled them to leave their families, professions, and security to turn the world upside down. He made the curse a gift.

For most of human history, men and women have used physical rites to guide them into spiritual realms, but our culture seems to have forgotten how to do this. We've swapped holy journeys for one-week vacations that fail to satisfy our souls.

The contemporary church seems to concentrate on teaching as the focal point for spiritual formation. In contrast, Jesus pioneered the practice of kingdom journey. Jesus came to it naturally. He was born into it. His parents had to leave the country when he was a baby in order to save his life. As a boy, he wandered from them during a family pilgrimage to Jerusalem. Finally, he left Nazareth for good.

What thoughts went through his head as he hung up his carpenter's apron for the last time and began his itinerant ministry? Did he experience the thrill that those of us who set out on a long trip often feel?

The first stop on Jesus' journey was the Jordan River to be baptized. Next, was a month in the desert where he faced the devil incarnate. His desert leg of the journey emphasized the principle of abandon. He had nothing to eat and no one to encourage him. The whole incident left him so wrung-out and exhausted that God sent angels to help him recuperate when it was finished.

Jesus wants us to follow his model: to imitate him. We're prone to dismiss it as quaint or anachronistic, but his pattern applies to us all. He left behind everything that felt like the comforts of home. He was taken to a place of brokenness and utter dependence on the Father. Along the way, God met his needs, as *he will meet our needs.* Jesus' ministry began with what was really an extended mission trip that morphed into a three-year kingdom journey.

At age thirty, Jesus left home and wandered from village to village until he arrived at Golgotha. Within that journey, he used smaller side trips to help his followers grow. Christ called his disciples and would-be disciples to join his journey — a call to that led to his brokenness and surrender — as well as theirs. He called them to changes that could only happen away from the familiarity of home. If you examine his mentorship, you can't escape this conclusion: *We can't be fully transformed in our own backyard. We need to journey.*

Jesus sent out his disciples in two waves. As reported in Matthew 10, Mark 6, and Luke 9, he first sent out "the twelve". He sent them with authority to drive out demons, cure sickness, and to deliver a message, "The kingdom is near." These were not regular excursions, not like a '60's road trip in a psychedelic VW microbus fueled by rebellion. Nor were these adventures mere voyages of self-discovery. They were journeys infused with a sense of the sacred. They were rites of initiation into the kingdom, holy expeditions where the disciples found themselves hidden in God.

Kingdom journeys always produce an increased return. In Luke 10, Jesus sent out seventy-two disciples. He sent them into the towns he was about to visit, as lambs among wolves. He sent them into conflict — not just with the world — but also within themselves.

These twelve Jesus sent out with the following instructions:

"As you go, proclaim this message, 'The kingdom of heaven has come near.' Heal the sick, raise the dead, cleanse those who have leprosy, drive out demons. Freely you have received; freely give."

"Do not get any gold or silver or copper to take with you in your belts — no bag for the journey or extra shirt or sandals or a staff…" (Matthew 10:7-10).

TOTAL ABANDON, TOTAL DEPENDENCE

This is how missions — whether long-term or short-term — can accelerate discipleship. If you were to look at the list of people who joined our trip to Peru in 2002, you'd notice that most of them are currently engaged in some kind of ministry leadership, either full-time or as a committed volunteer.

Some critics claim that short-term missions are a waste of time, money, and manpower. Short-term missions, they say, are a distraction to more legitimate forms of ministry. A prominent media-based ministry recently published a particularly harsh critique of short-term missions, pointing out that advocates say their programs encourage people to get involved in long-term missions. "However, according to a study by the American Society of Missiology," says the article, "that connection is not so clear. The study points out that while short-term missions have surged in the last twenty years, the number of new missionaries has actually declined."[17]

It's a fair point. Too many short-term-missions organizations do a poor job of planning and coordinating their trips. Far too many are more like spiritual vacations than Jesus-centered kingdom journeys. Good short-term missions, like that trip to Peru, usually last longer than a week. They focus on abandoning our cultural places of comfort for the places belonging to the poor, the lost, and the broken. Jesus-centered short-term missions, like the Matthew 10 and Luke 9-10 trips, focus on complete dependence on God.

In his list of twelve major spiritual disciplines, Richard Foster left one out. Although it existed before his ministry on earth, Jesus used it with tremendous effect. It is one of the oldest spiritual disciplines, and was instituted by God the Father himself. Yet, we have largely ignored it. We've been too small, too safe, and too provincial. We need to rediscover what God was doing when he sent out Abraham, Moses, Elijah, Jesus, and yes, even Jessi and Claud to discover the kingdom. Journey can be the means God uses to show you your true self. It's how God reshapes us. It is simply the best tool I've found to bring a generation fully alive.

Imagine if we put Jesus' trips in the terms of Shackleton's advertisement: "Men wanted for hazardous journey. Wages, provisions, uniforms strictly prohibited. Bitter enemies encountered everywhere. Long months of persecution, extreme hunger, and return doubtful. Eternal glory and treasure in case of success."[18] It has a certain ring to it, doesn't it?

CHAPTER 3 NOTES

11. Gordon McDonald, "Leader's Insight: So Many Christian Infants," *Leadership Journal*, http://www. christianitytoday.com/le/2007/october-online-only/ cln71001.html?start=2.

12. Jimmy Page and Robert Plant, "Stairway to Heaven" in *Led Zeppelin IV* (New York: Atlantic, 1971).

13. Bruce Springsteen, "Born to Run" in *Born to Run* (Los Angeles: CBS Records, 1975).

14. Dan Layrus, "Boston" in *All the Stars and Boulevards* (New York: Epic Records, 2005).

15. Jack Kerouac, *On the Road* (New York: Penguin Books, 1999), 7.

16. Joni Mitchell, "Rainy Night House" in *Ladies of the Canyon* (Burbank, California: Reprise Records, 1970).

17. Chuck Holton, "Are Short-Term Mission Trips Effective," *CBN News*, http://www.cbn.com/ cbnnews/569604.aspx.

18. Wikipedia,http://en.wikipedia.org/ wikiEndurance_%281912_ship%29.

CHAPTER 4: THE STAGES OF JOURNEY

"It is always our own self that we find at the end of the journey. The sooner we face that self, the better." — Ella Maillart[19]

Jessi Marquez had to confront the emptiness of her life when she asked for a week off from work to go to Australia. She had dreamt of it for years. Finally, Jessi saved enough money to pay for a vacation and asked Brenda, her boss, for a week away from work. A couple days before the conversation with Brenda, Jessi had a moment of desperation and loneliness. She came to realize she had no relationship with God. She wanted more than an escape, promising to give anything to have a relationship with Him.

"A week off? That's impossible," said Brenda. "Maybe in a couple of years, but you've got to put in your dues for a while." Jessi was speechless. She couldn't believe what she was hearing. She was going to have to wait another couple of *years* to go? Seeing her frustration, her boss tried to cheer her up. "Listen Jessi, if you keep working as hard as you do now, I promise: *someday* you'll be just like me."

Brenda was a New York City success story. She had a mansion in the Hamptons and a fancy apartment in Manhattan. Who wouldn't want that? Yet, Jessi understood how lonely and empty Brenda's life was. Jessi had no desire to be just like Brenda. That day, Jessi received the Gift of Restlessness. For the first time, she could see that the grass definitely *was* greener on the other side. After overhearing a conversation in Central Park about a trip called the World Race, Jessi made plans to quit her job and go, not merely on vacation, but on a kingdom journey.

Soon, Jessi was in the Red Light district in Malaysia. Her heart ached as American businessmen purchased Malay girls with pasted smiles and glazed over eyes. Jessi worked with a ministry dedicated to getting women out of prostitution. For a few dollars, these prostitutes would be anyone their customers wanted them to be.

Some of them even flirted with Jessi until she convinced them that she was only interested in being friends. Perhaps Jessi saw something of herself in them. She was also a city girl who would wear anything for a compliment, no matter the cost. She saw their humanity and their profound need for deliverance and salvation.

In the Philippines, Jessi visited the home of a single-mother and her nine children. "Home" is a misnomer; it was more like a shack. Two of the daughters were on the verge of being kicked out of school because they had been absent so many times. Their mother was too exhausted from raising four other small children to get them ready for school in the morning.

Jessi was there for three weeks. During that time she did not sleep in ritzy hotels. She did not sunbathe on the beaches nor shop at outdoor markets. Instead, she walked the girls to school. She cleaned up Nestle, the three-year-old boy who ran around naked and covered in dirt. Jessi held the mother's two-month-old baby, so small and malnourished that she fit in the palms of Jessi's hands.

Later, Jessi went to Kenya, where she met Anna, a Tutsi woman who had survived the Rwandan genocide by the Hutus. When the Hutus came for Anna, she took refuge in a church, along with her mother and siblings. Anna told Jessi how the Hutus slaughtered adults and children; how they raped her mother and sisters in front of her; how they cut open her mother's uterus (she was seven months pregnant), and threw the unborn child against a wall while her mother bled to death. Anna recounted how they killed her brothers and sisters while she watched, hidden and helpless behind a curtain.

Afterward, Jessi wrote, "It is when people don't allow God to show up through them that the world collapses in on itself."

Jessi wasn't in Manhattan, anymore.

WHAT IS A KINGDOM JOURNEY?

Jessi's kingdom journey was uniquely her own, yet it looked like so many others. Kingdom journeys may differ in their details, but share similar stages. The two-month kingdom journey to Guatemala may take you down the same spiritual road as the two-year Peace Corps trip to Burundi. They all involve a commitment to go. The difference is *why* you go, *what* you do when you get there, and *how* your life changes because of the journey.

The Wall Street Journal reporter, Sue Shellenbarger, notes that more students are taking a year off from school — often called a "gap year" — for recovery and enrichment. "Gap-year activities range from doing volunteer work or taking classes," she says, "to working for pay, traveling or tackling outdoor adventures."[20] Gap years can be memorable, but they aren't the same as kingdom journeys.

What sets a kingdom journey apart from gap years, road trips, and volunteer jaunts is the central focus on Jesus' kingdom. A kingdom journey is first and foremost about expanding God's reign in the world and increasing it inside our hearts.

To understand what transforms an ordinary trip into a *kingdom* journey, we need to look at Jesus. Early in his ministry, he chose men and sent them out into the villages of Judea. "Go!" he said to them. "I am sending you out like lambs among wolves." In case they thought he was joking, he told them to take no money, no extra clothes, and no shoes. When was the last time you heard a message like this given from the pulpit? Such an assignment may have worked in Jesus' day, but who could dare something so radical today?

YOU MIGHT BE SURPRISED

All over the world, young people with little to lose *are* making such voyages. Andrew Maas, for example, rode his bike from Florida to Texas with nothing but a water bottle and a Bible. David Hepting and three of his friends did the same, biking two hundred miles through Kenya — from Eldoret to Nakuru and back.

In the spirit of Luke 10, others are on similar excursions, circling the globe with only a backpack, a tent, and a sleeping pad. They leave their homes, motivated by the prospect of finding something bigger than them — something that will help them make sense of their existence. They are seeking the kingdom of God, whether they know it or not.

Wherever Jesus' disciples walked, they were looking for the kingdom. Whoever they talked to, they were looking for a sign of the kingdom. Much to their amazement, the kingdom *did* come. But it didn't come through a place or an event; *it came through a people.*

Kingdom journey is based on Jesus' example. It is about expanding God's reign in the world and increasing it inside our own hearts. Jesus sent his disciples on a journey to find the kingdom. They discovered the kingdom right where God put it — *inside* them.

WHY A JOURNEY?

Maybe you're wondering, "Why should I go on a trip halfway around the world to find the kingdom of God if it's already inside me?" Good question. The short answer is: *You need to go not for the destination or for the mileage on your odometer, but for what God shows you along the way.* I personally had to go to Peru to understand the importance of depending on God.

I'm an animal lover. The first pet I ever owned was a guinea pig named Calico. An older couple I was visiting in Peru kept a menagerie of animals: dozens of pigeons, ducks, dogs, and about fifty guinea pigs. When we sat down for our evening meal, Our hostess had lovingly prepared a feast in our honor which included a platter of four of her finest whole-roasted guinea pigs! You could still see their little front teeth and whiskers. As we gingerly nibbled the greasy skin of the guinea pigs, the hostess watched us, making sure we were enjoying her cooking. It was all we could do to smile and swallow.

God has been getting me through uncomfortable places ever since. Through discomfort, I've learned to depend on God when my natural instinct is to rely on my own skills and talents.

We organize our lives around maximizing our comfort and control. Sitting down to a meal of roast childhood pet showed me that a good kingdom journey takes you to places where you are not in control. Kingdom journeys force us to depend on God to help us regain our sense of balance. You find out very quickly that the standard bag of tricks you use to get your way and to maintain your comfort zone is useless in places like Peru.

We go to work, endure traffic, eat our breakfast, lunch and dinner; and go to bed at the same time every day. Routine is normal, even healthy, but if the ruts go too deep, our spirits begin to whither. If we never get out of our comfort zones, we can't grow into the places God has prepared for us.

To combat this comfort-seeking tendency in his disciples, Jesus routinely destabilized them. Jesus asked his followers to leave everything for a season so they might learn to see with spiritual eyes for their entire lives. They went on a journey that threw them out of their comfort zones and forced them to depend on God. He didn't grow his disciples in classrooms, but in the hard-knocks of real life. He moved them from place to place to help them lose their bearings and disrupt the predictable. Slowly, they changed from comfort-seekers to kingdom-minded citizens of heaven.

It took a roasted guinea pig to teach me that God would not neatly fit inside the cultural box I had welded for him. I realized that my comfort zone is a poor place to ask God to live. I learned that God didn't look like me or have the same cultural prejudices as I did. I learned to become more tolerant — of him and his people. I even ate guinea pig. Who knew?

Where did I find God's kingdom during my journey to Peru? I found it being built right inside of me. I never would have learned that lesson if I hadn't gotten in that yellow Vega years before to begin my kingdom journey.

AMONGST THE ADDICTS

Claud Crosby felt God calling him to drop out of school to go on his kingdom journey. Although the call he heard was clear, he still felt pressured to stay. Even though he was bored at college and had been to three schools in two years, he was afraid of leaving. The summer after his sophomore year, Claud left his home in a rich suburb in Virginia for his grandfather's little beach house on the coast. He got a job at a marina scraping barnacles off of boats. He was alone for nearly forty days, and during that time, he wrestled with God. Claud knew the Lord wanted him to abandon everything familiar to go on a kingdom journey, but he wasn't ready. Even though he was apathetic toward school, he had an easy, comfortable life with good friends and a serious girlfriend.

After his time alone with God, Claud left the coast having decided to ignore God's call and go back to school. "I couldn't open the Word for three weeks," he said. "I knew exactly what he was going to say, and I didn't want to hear it." Finally, he couldn't take it anymore. He sat down with his Bible. "As soon as I opened it, I just started bawling." With that, he dropped out of school, said goodbye to his friends, and broke up with his girlfriend. Tough decisions, but ones he knew were right.

A month later, he was on the streets of inner-city Philadelphia, ministering to drug addicts and prostitutes. "Some of the guys we worked with were doing eighteen bags of heroin a day," said Claud. "$180 a day. Most of them got the money by stealing. You have to do some pretty serious theft to get $180 a day."

Claud ministered in Philly for two years, working and living in community with other young people who were pursuing an equally radical walk with God. A missionary named Dave Hain discipled him. Dave's story inspired Claud to abandon everything he knew and loved for God's Kingdom. Dave had been a top executive at a national corporation before Jesus met him in his hotel room on a business trip. He had abandoned his ladder-climbing life to serve the poor in the inner city.

A few years later, Claud was in a hospital in Swaziland feeding a baby that had been found in the forest. Linlobo Nondumiso was just a day old. Her umbilical cord was still attached. Everyone wondered how she hadn't died, since there was no one to feed her in the forest. A bottle had been found on the ground next to her. Evidently, if she moved her head, she was able to feed herself.

As Claud picked up Nondumiso and placed a bottle in her mouth, a nurse asked, "Are you going to take your daughter home today?" "No, she's not mine," Claud said. God then spoke to him, "This *is* your daughter."

It was a lot to absorb, but he and his wife, Mary, sensed God confirming what he'd shown them. So they began the adoption process. Less than a month later they brought Nondumiso — now their beloved daughter — home.

Claud and Jessi were each on a kingdom journey. Claud's began in the United States. He spent several years in a single place before moving on. Altogether, it lasted nearly eight years. Jessi's journey lasted a year, and she spent only a month in each location. As different as their journeys were, they answered several common questions:

- How long should a kingdom journey last?

- Do you have to leave the country?

- Do you have to move around all the time or can you stay in one place?

SMASHING THE GOD BOX

A kingdom journey smashes the boxes we try to put God in. We tend to think that God only acts in certain ways because that's all we've experienced. Look at the disciples. Jesus sent them out with no money, no clothes, and no shoes. They had seen Jesus do miracles, but their faith still wavered. As uneducated peasants, they lived under the foot of the Romans, the most powerful empire in the history of the world. Yet, after their kingdom journey, they returned saying, "Even the demons submit to us in your name" (Luke 10:17).

Questions about the length or extent of a journey can miss the point. We aren't told how long the journeys in Luke 9 and 10 actually lasted. Perhaps it will take a journey of week, or maybe several months or more to rock your world. Sometimes our questions about structure result from our need for control or our desire to take the mystery out of the mysterious. Men like Abraham, Jesus, and Paul embraced mystery. All went on a kingdom journey. Their experience poses some alternative questions:

- Does God want *me* to go on a kingdom journey?

- Where does he want me to go?

- How long does he want me to commit to the journey?

- Who will go with me?

- Who will coach me through it?

THE THREE STAGES

Jessi and Claud left everything and immersed themselves in meaningful Kingdom work. Along the way, they learned that a kingdom journey often works best in another culture — even another continent. Why? Because God has to teach his disciples new ways to communicate, survive, and thrive. Jessi and Claud left to experience the powerful **first** stage of kingdom journey, **Abandonment.**

Claud's kingdom journey began when he abandoned his comfortable home in the Richmond suburbs for the streets in Philly. Later, he lived in Swaziland and South Africa; doing community development with thousands of AIDS orphans. This wasn't a Saturday afternoon ministry opportunity. Claud abandoned the lifestyle that had defined him before. He learned the lifestyle of ministry rather than compartmentalizing ministry into an already-packed schedule. He left his family and friends and creature comforts and discovered new friends along the way.

Brokenness, the **second** stage of kingdom journey takes you to your broken places and enables you to embrace them. Claud and Jessi both knew they needed to change. They were also vulnerable enough to admit they couldn't change themselves. Their hearts were broken for the poor and it made them less selfish. Coming face-to-face with the world's needs forced Jessi and Claud to confront their narcissistic tendency to focus on their own needs. They realized that if they were comparatively rich, they should give to those in need.

Did life suddenly become easy when they left home? No, the truth is life became a lot harder. They couldn't cover up their brokenness with the same old easy fixes. One day in a mall in Thailand, Jessi had an anxiety attack. She paced through the mall for four hours, looking at all the cute bows, sneakers, and skinny jeans. She was convinced she "needed" these things. "Stuff" had become an addiction. Clothes made her feel pretty whenever she felt depressed. Who needs to rely on God when a new outfit will suffice?

It took a kingdom journey to put her feelings into a godly perspective. Jessi learned why she felt lonely and why she responded in a worldly way. Armed with insight and resolve, she embraced a new identity that is free from dependence upon possessions. Jessi discovered a new identity in Christ formed in cultures and countries far away from her own.

This kind of honest soul-searching is something you see in the brokenness stage. When you are truly broken, authenticity is all you have left. You're motivated to find something solid in your interior life to anchor to. For a spiritual discipline to be worthwhile, it must create space for God to change us from the inside out.

YOU CAN'T BE REMADE UNTIL YOU FIRST ALLOW YOURSELF TO BE UNMADE.

The **third** stage, Claud and Jessi learned, is **Dependence**. It flows easily from brokenness. When your life no longer works, all you have left is God. Because what once worked is broken — because you're no longer self-sufficient — you have to depend on God.

One day, Dave sent Claud on a prayer walk in the city. Along the way, Claud had the distinct impression that God was telling him to go into a shop, but when he saw what kind of shop it was, he balked. "A Philly cheese-steak shop?" he thought. "Really God? That's not what I'm here for!" When the feeling persisted, he finally surrendered and went in. Moments after he moved, two men started shooting at each other right where he had been standing. He *would have been* in their line of fire. But he obeyed and moved out of unseen danger. After that, dependence on God made more sense than ever!

During her month-long kingdom journey, Jessi sensed God leading her to carry only a tiny daypack. She could only take three T-shirts, one pair of jeans, a pair of shorts, and a skirt. For a girl whose wardrobe had been her identity, this was a total makeover by God himself. A transformation such as Jessi's is best made while on a kingdom journey, where it's made from the inside out.

You can't be remade until you first allow yourself to be unmade. Nothing forces that upon you quite like a kingdom journey, where God is all you have left and your reliance on him is absolute. You see that you were never really self-sufficient, no matter how much you prized independence.

Jesus sent his disciples on a kingdom journey. They were never the same; neither was the world around them. Do you want to change the world? You can begin, by God's grace.

Recognize that the first three steps down the path of changing the world will be costly:

1. Abandon your comfort zone
2. Embrace your brokenness
3. Depend on God

What follows will take you to the edge of yourself and leave you a new person. You may never want to repeat the journey, but it may well be the most important thing you will have ever accomplished.

CHAPTER 4 NOTES

19. Quoted in BrainyQuote.com, *Ella Maillart Quotes*, http://www.brainyquote.com/quotes/authors/e/ella_maillart.html.

20. Sue Shellenbarger, "Delaying College to Fill in the Gaps," *Wall Street Journal*, online.wsj.com/article/SB1000 14240529702035132045760477239222275698.html.

CHAPTER 5: ABANDON

"An adventure is only an inconvenience rightly considered. An inconvenience is only an adventure wrongly considered"
— G.K. Chesterton[21]

Jesus wasn't my only inspiration to leave, though his example fueled my imagination. It was a whisper I heard deep within my spirit calling me out of the familiar and into adventure.

At some point in our lives, we are all called into the unknown. We have a choice: to ignore the call or to obey it. If we are obedient, we will find ourselves wholly depending upon God, but it will not be easy. It will be anything but comfortable.

When Jesus first called his disciples to go on their journey of abandonment, he launched them into a hot and dangerous countryside. It was a violent land full of suspicious people, a country accustomed to invasions and war. Not a great place to start a movement nor a great environment to go wandering about.

His packing list left much to be desired:

- No money

- No traveler's bag

- No change of clothes

- No shoes

- No walking stick

Jesus had a point to make. He was already preaching a kingdom that stood logic on its head — the first shall be last, the poor in spirit will be blessed, love your enemy, and pray for those who do you wrong. Jesus knew we would never learn to rely on God unless we walked away from the crutches we're prone to lean on.

Just the physical act of leaving brings about spiritual fruit. We learn to depend on his Spirit by breaking unhealthy habits and addictive comforts. Learning to leave is how we find our true selves.

In 2010, Marlena Griffey was graduating from Texas A&M. She pursued her version of the American Dream: "a good job, a decent income, a husband, and a white picket fence." When Marlena was in high school, things were different. She felt God calling her to be a missionary. She even spent a summer in a Mayan village in the Yucatan jungle teaching English and sharing the Gospel. She wanted to believe that visit fulfilled God's direction to "go to the nations," that her summer as a missionary fulfilled God's call on her life.

Marlena planned to become a teacher. She spent the last year of college as a teacher's assistant for first-graders and loved it. Her life was headed in the direction of stability and success. But God had other plans. "One word that was whispered in my ear," she said, "over and over for months, maybe even years, was: '*Leave.*'"

The sound of abandonment echoed in Marlena's soul like a constant drip from a broken faucet. She couldn't get rid of it. It just kept getting louder. "Life has not worked itself into a nice, neat little plan. It has not pushed me toward a career, a place close to home, a wedding. I am at this crossroad. One signpost reads, 'Comfortable living.' The other says: *'Leave.'*"

Leaving meant she would miss her friends, family, boyfriend, and her familiar life. She would enter a world of instability where unknowns lurked everywhere. She felt as if the unknown *itself* was calling to her to leave home, as if abandon itself was whispering in her ear. Was it God? Or was it something else?

PACK LIGHT

What Marlena experienced was the same calling and urging the first disciples struggled with. Jesus intended for his disciples to actually have *less* than they needed to survive. He told them to take nothing but the Kingdom with them, "Do not take a purse or bag or sandals" (Luke 10:4). What appeared to be reckless behavior brought them newness of life in the kingdom of God. They learned to believe that the Father would provide for them. He did, of course.

I asked Matt Snyder, a young writer and musician from Kansas, how he felt after his kingdom journey. Matt left on a year-long mission with our organization in 2008. In Malawi, he was asked to preach for ten days straight. He faced his fears, - daily speaking to huge gatherings - sometimes even to senior leaders in churches. Although nerve-racking, the experience was a highlight of his trip. Why? Because his journey taught him to abandon self-consciousness. He could only learn this through the physical act of standing up in front of an audience and speaking — the last thing he wanted to do.

Abandoning self-consciousness was just one of many things God asked Matt to do. While he and his team were driving from Malawi to South Africa, their truck broke down. A truck breaking down in the States is bad enough, but in a foreign country where very few speak English, it can be a disaster. The team was stranded for four days.

Another time, Matt was returning to his hostel in South Africa when a taxi driver named Joe started asking him questions about Jesus. He answered as best as he could, but felt inadequate. "I am by no means an evangelist," he wrote to me later, "but I'm trying to get better about sharing Jesus' love with people through words." A month later, he saw the taxi driver again. As he talked to him, Matt was thrilled to see Joe had given his life to God.

Later, Matt and his team were robbed at gunpoint. His laptop was stolen, along with most of his clothes.

One way to look at this would be to say, "What a disastrous trip! You're lucky you survived." Matt, however, had a different outlook. When asked how he felt after a year of challenges, Matt said, "Hands down, I'm more awake, more alive. The man that God had always created me to become was finally resurrected. I'm no longer a walking dead man. I'm a man fully alive!"

How does leaving everything behind make people more alive? It's a paradox. Abandoning the things that make you comfortable can leave you careening along a roller coaster of emotion. "It was both the most difficult and the richest time of my life," remembers Claud Crosby. "I was ecstatic about what was happening inside of me." The process of abandoning is exhausting and exciting. Even the most ordinary experiences — eating, sleeping, and going to the bathroom — are new and unusual.

Simply surviving can be uncomfortable at times. When you lose your routine, you lose control. Abandoning your safe, little world makes you vulnerable. In this sense, you become like a child again. Everything seems new again. By leaving what we trust and know, we begin to trust and know new things. We learn to rely on a Father who does not abandon his children, to really open ourselves up to his love. Ultimately, we learn to obey as we never have before.

Becoming a child again is exactly what God wants. This is the point of abandoning. He wants us to look at the world through new eyes, eyes that see beauty and joy and excitement in all things, even the most ordinary of circumstances. He wants us to give up our control and to trust him. Abandoning reminds us to be childlike in the middle of life at a time when we've long forgotten what it's like to be a child. This is why we leave; it's why we go on a journey in the first place.

As part of the abandonment process, God asks us to give up control and remain open to new things. We leave as an act of obedience so we can learn to depend more on God, allowing him to increase our spiritual vision. Jesus said that when the eyes are healthy, the whole body is full of light (Luke 11:34). Abandonment causes our eyes to open wide.

TRAVELING COMPANIONS

Before abandonment finishes its work, people feel lonely and disconnected. We wonder, "What if I never make it back to a place of comfort? Will abandoning everything, and everyone, only make me more lonely, restless, and anxious?" We need some measure of comfort to navigate life.

Given that the cost of a journey can be emotionally staggering, how can we practice abandon in a time like this? How can we go on a kingdom journey at all when the emotional health in our culture seems on the wane? Shouldn't we instead be hunkering down, trying to improve our relationships - if not for ourselves, at least for all the others who struggle with debilitating loneliness? If we have the chance to help, why would we even think about abandoning everything?

America Ferrera, star of the television show, *Ugly Betty*, recounts a time when she was nineteen and shooting a movie in Utah. The movie paid very well, and she had more money than ever before. She was completely free to do whatever she wanted; yet, she was incredibly lonely. "I couldn't step outside of my loneliness no matter how much money I had." She called her sister, flew her out to Utah, and wasn't lonely anymore.[22]

What are we to do when we encounter loneliness in the desert where God leads us? For one thing, we know that journeys are usually better in the company of others. We need community and we do better if we find people to journey with us. Humans have a need to be known at a deep emotional level. Having a million superficial friendships can feel the same as having none.

Journeys with fellow believers create lifelong and eternal bonds. David Brooks, a columnist for The New York Times, says: "Research over the past thirty years makes it clear that what the inner mind really wants is connection. *It's a Wonderful Life* was right."[23] Jobs that are primarily social, according to Brooks, bring the most happiness. Being part of a group that meets regularly increases happiness at the same level as a 100% raise in pay. Relationships, not freedom, bring us happiness. Is this not even truer in the community of faith?

INITIATION

The kingdom journeys Jesus sent his disciples on in Luke 9 and 10 are examples of initiation rites. They challenged disciples to look for something deeper than their own personal advancement — a larger purpose than the American Dream.

In the West, we have the assumption that young people naturally grow up to become normal socially conscious adults. Yet, preindustrial societies knew that young people, especially young men, needed to be *made* into adults.

In *Adam's Return*, Richard Rohr, a Franciscan monk who has studied initiation for years, writes about a phenomenon among elephants in Africa. A group of young males were acting strangely, "They were stomping on VWs, pushing over trees for no reason, and even killing other small animals and baby elephants." What was going on with these young males? They were acting like an inner-city gang.

Scientists studied the elephants and realized they had no older males in the herd, probably because they had been poached for their tusks. Their solution was simple. The scientists flew in a few older males and the young elephants soon calmed down.

"Apparently, all the old bulls did was wave their ears," says Rohr. "Somehow, the younger male elephants understood ... that their behavior was not the way good elephant boys should act." These young males had to be shown how to become adults, and for thousands of years, most human cultures did the same.

Rohr says young people who aren't initiated will find a way to do it themselves: "Today, young men try to self-initiate by pushing themselves to the edges and into risk in various ways. The instinct for initiation is still there."[24]

Think of the movie series, *Jackass,* where young men paper-cut the corners of their mouths or put fishhooks through their cheeks. Something inside of them is craving initiation. It manifests as a need to take risks. And that's exactly what young people get when they abandon their comforts and leave on a kingdom journey.

In order to experience life as it was meant to be lived, we must leave. There is no other way. It's a form of fasting. Just as when we fast from food we grow spiritually, so we grow in our spiritual lives when we abandon other creature comforts in our physical lives. There is fruit that must be borne inside of us, fruit that shows up when we experience discomfort.

There is a profound connection between our spirits and bodies. We weren't meant to separate the two. We must *go* to connect them once again. To understand the kingdom, we must receive eyes that see the world differently. There is a kingdom to discover that will not come to you. To experience it for yourself, you must leave. You must abandon. You must *go.*

CHAPTER 5 NOTES

21. Quoted in The Quotations Page, http://www.
thequotationspage.com/quote/26278.html.

22. Jesse Sweet and Daniel Gilbert, *PBS: This Emotional
Life,* television series segment, Boston: WGBH, premiered
September 2009.

23. David Brooks, "Social Animal: How the New
Sciences of Human Nature can Help Make Sense of
Life," *The New Yorker,* http://www.newyorker.com/
reporting/2011/01/17/110117fa_fact_brooks.

24. Richard Rohr, *Adam's Return: The Five Promises
of Male Initiation,* (New York: Crossroad Publishing
Company, 2004), 11-12.

CHAPTER 6: THE SPIRITUAL ACT OF ABANDONMENT

It is only in adventure that some people succeed in knowing themselves - in finding themselves. — André Gide[25]

The leaving process has almost always been complicated and often unpleasant for me. I can't think of any journey I took away from loved ones that didn't begin with tears. Accustomed to their presence and to the comforts of home, I've grown wary of the effort it takes to actually leave.

I've learned that it's normal to misinterpret what God is doing along the way. Although I'd begun the abandoning process by leaving home and family at twenty-one, it wasn't until ten years later, when I lost my job — and my sense of success — that I completed the process of abandoning. For a long time, I looked at the pain that attended this stripping away as a misstep on the journey — or perhaps a punishment. Instead of appreciating what God was doing in my life, I recited the script of a victim and focused blame on the people he'd used as tools to do his work in me.

Only later in life have I seen how universal my experience is. I look around and others are struggling through variations of my journey. Tiffany Berkowitz is a good example. She's my children's age, but her journey mirrors my own. Tiffany was a children's director at a San Diego mega-church. Leadership included perks.

"At this church," she said, "there were always people around me, people wanting to be my friend, people wanting to do stuff with me." She was the pillar of a large social group, but that wasn't enough. "I was restless. I remember feeling really lonely." She tried to fix her dissatisfaction in different ways, to no avail. "One time, it was a guy. Another time, I started a ministry. Another time, I went out." Her job began to feel shallow. "Doing ministry was a paycheck," she recalled. She kept looking for people who felt the same way she did. She wanted to experience a deeper level of intimacy. "The whole church revolved around *doing*. It was what every message was about. I can't recall a single message about being in relationship with the Lord," she said.

Then, she met someone who had gone on a kingdom journey. "I remember it sounding raw ... not just a fluffy missions trip," Tiffany said. "I remember thinking, maybe this is what I'm looking for."

A few months after signing up, she left for Guatemala, leaving her church, her social circle, and boyfriend. All because she sensed God had something better for her.

Was Tiffany just another girl looking for greener pastures, another dissatisfied young person? Would she really be any less lonely on the road than in San Diego? She began to have doubts. She had anxiety attacks when she thought about the year of abandonment that lay ahead. "Everything 'great' was taken out of my hands," she said. "I was either trading it for something better or something psychotic ... I had no clue what I was getting myself into."

LEAVING FRIENDS

Tiffany worried that leaving everything was crazy. Anthropologist Victor Turner would have said it was necessary. Observing initiation rites in the Ndembu people, Turner noted the intense sense of camaraderie initiates felt with one another. Their connection was strengthened as they bonded together by shared experience. When they returned to the village, their kinship ties deepened. They were more interested in learning from elders and willing to take care of them. These rites of passage were the glue of the community. Turner called this phenomenon *communitas*, and defined it as "an intense communal spirit that forms as a result of these rites of passage ceremonies."[26]

For the Christian, *communitas* resembles the spirit of the early church, where people sold their belongings and gave to the church body. In Acts 2, the poor were literally blessed, as Jesus promised, because of the communal life of the church. They saw themselves as equals. They were each other's brothers and sisters. They used their gifts for the good of the community.

The point? There is a finding in the leaving. Generally speaking, people shouldn't go out on a kingdom journey alone. Jesus sent the disciples out in pairs. Our ministry sends people out in groups of six. The community formed in these groups is amazing.

Ruth Wilson reflected on the first month of her kingdom journey:

"My idea of community for most of my life has been going to a Bible study once a week. If I was ever uncomfortable, I would stop going. This community does not work like that. You wake up in the morning next to community. All day long, community notices every time you roll your eyes. Community will not be escaped. Living in community is the scariest, hardest, most out of control, beautiful thing I have ever been through in my life."

My son, Seth Jr., observed a similar dynamic with his team, "We all know each other's tendencies, insecurities, wounds, and limitations. We've all got our stuff. This is what community is all about — joining a tribe on a journey through death to life."

C.S. Lewis says, "Our Lord finds our desires not too strong, but too weak. We are half-hearted creatures, fooling about with drink and sex and ambition when infinite joy is offered us, like an ignorant child who wants to go on making mud pies in a slum because he cannot imagine what is meant by the offer of a holiday at the sea. We are far too easily pleased."[27]

Abandonment is about discarding weak desire: shallow community, superficial prayers, and boring religion. Instead of praying, "Thank you, Father, for this food," we pray, "Thank you, Father, that you didn't give us food today. Instead, today, *you* will be our food." Abandonment is the business of discarding lowlier desires so that we discover a true desire for God. It's a beautiful exchange.

When Jesus called his disciples to join him on a journey, he was teaching them they would have nothing to depend on — no stable jobs, no place to sleep, no guaranteed meals —

nothing, but each other. In leaving, we can connect with God through others. Abandonment is a means to an end; a deeper connection to what a heart longs for.

WHAT TO LEAVE

A physical journey parallels the deeper spiritual journey. What do we really need to leave? While there are many things to leave, perhaps most important is that we leave ourselves.

Keturah Weathers, a young woman from California, was struck by the Gift of Restlessness in college. She had to pick a major, but couldn't. The problem wasn't that she didn't enjoy her studies. She liked every class she took, but never fell in love with any of the subjects. She also didn't want to be personally defined by a career path in any of those fields:

> "I would get excited about a certain major for a while, but my thoughts would always fall back to, '*Is that it? If I pick this, is that gonna be what the rest of my life looks like?* None of it looks satisfying. Everything seems self-involved, empty, and ultimately unfulfilling.'"

After college, Keturah's life started to slide out of control. She hit a personal rock bottom, feeling she was "failing at life." To escape the shame, she quit everything: jobs, boyfriend, even school. Her actions hint at the difference between

A PHYSICAL JOURNEY PARALLELS THE DEEPER SPIRITUAL JOURNEY.

abandonment and escapism. Keturah wasn't leaving everything for community, healing, or initiation — or God. She was quitting because life got too hard. However, this brought her to a place where she could begin to confront her issues.

At a weekend retreat, she was touched by God's love for the first time. Soon afterward, God called Keturah on a kingdom journey. In order to leave, she needed to abandon some nasty habits and an unhealthy environment. More than that, she needed to "quit" the idea that God didn't love her. She needed to abandon not just her sins, but also her understanding of who God was and the box she'd put him in.

THE FALSE SELF

Abandonment is the process of taking our hands off of what we have been holding onto. It involves turning away from lesser things and renouncing our "rights" to them. It is an emptying that clears away emotional space for new attachments. Going through this stage was particularly hard on Nicole Marrett. She had to give up her core understanding of herself.

Nicole, a native Texan, felt God calling her in college to go on a kingdom journey. But instead of dropping everything to follow God, she went to New York where she interned for a big fashion house. She planned to finish her internship, and then go to work for a fashion magazine. She was determined to love city living. Instead, she felt drained and lifeless. Four months later, she returned to Texas. Again, her kingdom journey loomed at the edge of her consciousness, but she fought it. She started applying for jobs around Texas and New York, but couldn't shake the idea of leaving. "Others have fun stories about 'the call,'" she said. "Mine wasn't a call. Try a deafening shout, followed by running. Lots of running."

Finally, Nicole gave in and decided to go on a kingdom journey. The problem was she had lots of clothes, makeup, and beauty appliances. She didn't know how she was going to get everything she "needed" into one backpack light enough to carry. Over time, what she considered to be a necessity changed. She packed enough Q-tips to last a year. She gave up comforts that many people in the world don't even know existed. "I use brow powder, for goodness sake," she said. "I'm pretty sure I'm the only person who feels like she can't live without *that* for a year."

Nicole's addiction to makeup wasn't the real problem. It was symptomatic of a deeper issue, her need to be in control. Her kingdom journey made this difficult. She gained eighteen pounds from a carbohydrate-heavy diet and grew insecure about her physical appearance. In Uganda, she sensed God telling her to do the unthinkable: *Fast from makeup for thirty days.* Prior to the fast, the longest Nicole had gone without makeup was three days. It was part of her identity. Now, she had to abandon her mask and reveal her insecurities for God to heal her heart.

A journey also helps us leave behind our sense of control. Our dependence on "masks" can cause us to create a false self. We see this all the time in television sitcoms or movies. George Costanza from *Seinfeld* is a case study in insecurity. He is a man perpetually in search of an ego boost. In *Meet the Parents,* Greg Focker is insecure around his father-in-law-to-be, which causes him to act in laughably awkward ways. We laugh because we've all felt like that. We relate to his need to pretend to be someone he's not. Nicole's false self was the mask of makeup; she needed it to feel beautiful. "I spent a lot of time grieving my 'old life,'" she said.

NARCISSISM NEEDS TO DIE

We parents just want the best for our children and we have tried to provide the best of everything for them. But too late, we're seeing our good intentions backfire. Young people are more self-referential, more narcissistic than ever before. Empathy is an antidote to narcissism. A good indicator is that today's college students are not as empathetic as college students of the 1980s and 1990s, as a recent University of Michigan study shows. "We found the biggest drop in empathy after the year 2000," said Sara Konrath, a researcher at the U-M Institute for Social Research. "College kids today are about 40 percent lower in empathy than their counterparts of twenty or thirty years ago, as measured by standard tests of this personality trait."[28]

"It's all about you" is a great worship song, but the reality is that we've raised a generation to believe "It's all about **ME**." In a thousand ways, we parents have raised them to defy Copernican logic by being the center of the universe.

The book, *The Narcissism Epidemic* states that nearly 10 percent of twenty-somethings have already experienced symptoms of narcissistic personality disorder; three times that of previous generations.[29] Thirty-percent believe they deserve a B just for showing up to class. Their tolerance for pain is minimal[30]; we Baby Boomers raised them in protective bubbles that leave them poorly prepared for the rough and tumble of real life.

People need pain to grow. So much of spiritual maturity has to do with how we process pain. Discipline entails embracing the painful or unpleasant in the short term in order to realize long-term gains. Though well intentioned, parents have deprived their children of this essential resource.

LEAVING OUR OLD SELVES

Our old lives — our old *selves* — get in the way of the new self that God is creating in us. To live, we need to abandon the false self and go on a journey to find who we really are. This is the hardest part of abandonment: exposing and discarding the false self. Nicole only discovered the extent of her addiction to makeup when she was faced with the prospect of abandoning it. We become so accustomed to our masks that we don't know what it's like to go without them. In fact, many of our masks may be cultural in origin. We are blind to them because everyone around us is wearing them.

This is one reason why a kingdom journey can be so effective in helping us discover our true self. Travel, especially in foreign places, helps us see with new eyes. When we abandon our habits, culture, and "needs," we are able to better see to the core of ourselves — seeing our true self.

A kingdom journey is most effective when we abandon what we think we cannot abandon. With less, we discover the core of who we are. Our true self emerges from the rubble of the false self.

Sterling Hayden, an actor who became a member of the CIA during World War II, experienced this idea of personal transformation through a journey. He worked in the film industry mainly to pay for his voyages around the world. He said this about leaving:

> "To be truly challenging, a voyage, like a life, must rest on a firm foundation of financial unrest. Otherwise, you are doomed to a routine traverse, the kind known to yachtsmen who play with their boats at sea.

Cruising, it is called. If you are contemplating a voyage and you have the means, abandon the venture until your fortunes change. Only then will you know what the sea is all about.

"I've always wanted to sail to the South Seas, but I can't afford it." What these men can't afford is not to go. They are enmeshed in the cancerous discipline of security. In the worship of security we fling our lives beneath the wheels of routine — and before we know it our lives are gone. What does a man need — really need? A few pounds of food each day, heat and shelter; six feet to lie down in — and some form of working activity that will yield a sense of accomplishment. That's all — in the material sense, and we know it."[31]

Similarly, only when we abandon in a way that scares us will we know what God is all about. On the World Race — our ministry's version of a kingdom journey — people can take as much as they can fit in a backpack, but even that is sometimes too much. Most people don't realize how little they actually need. I ask people getting back from their yearlong trip if they could have gone with less. Almost always, they say yes. Some would have bought 40-liter packs instead of 70-liter ones. They would have taken fewer clothes, fewer batteries, and no extra rolls of toilet paper.

Less is more on a kingdom journey. Less gets you to brokenness and dependence faster. Less allows God to reveal himself in weakness. Take less than you think you need. You'll find that your real needs are a lot smaller and different than you thought.

IS IT SAFE?

Some worry that this kind of abandonment — the kind that Jesus taught — is too dangerous. They wonder, "Is it safe?" But Jesus never promised safety. A better question to ask is, "Is the fruit worth the risk?"

In 1990, without telling anyone, Christopher McCandless abandoned his home in an upscale suburb of Washington, D.C. He left behind his school — Atlanta's prestigious Emory University — his family, and all of his possessions. He donated the sum of his bank account, $24,000, to a charity that fights starvation. Then he took to the road in an old, yellow Datsun. To commemorate his new identity as a wanderer, he chose for himself a new name, Alexander Supertramp.

The book, Into the Wild, tracks McCandless' progress as he abandoned everything, wandered the West, ate off the land and from the generosity of strangers; and slept under pine trees and highway overpasses. Eventually, he left civilization entirely for the Alaskan wilderness.

Jon Krakauer, his biographer, describes this abandonment, "At long last he was unencumbered, emancipated from the stifling world of his parents and peers...a world in which he felt grievously cut off from the raw throb of existence."[32]

In Alaska, he lived off game that he hunted with a .22 rifle. Several months into his journey, he became sick and grew too weak to hunt. After surviving an impressive 100 days in the wilderness, his body began to give in to starvation. The day before he died, he said, "I have had a happy life and thank the Lord," he wrote. "Goodbye and may God bless all!"[33]

Though it wasn't a kingdom journey, Alex McCandless' example is a story of abandon, albeit a flawed one. He was able to forsake his physical comfort for a deeper sense of purpose. To most of us, Alex's journey seems crazy. He left without telling anyone. He burned his money and went days without eating. His lifestyle wasn't just uncomfortable; it was foolhardy. Is this the kind of abandonment that a kingdom journey requires?

Leaving, to some, may seem less like trusting God and more like looking for danger. Young travelers Jessi Marquez and Matt Snyder were both robbed at gunpoint. Claud Crosby was in Kampala, Uganda, when suicide bombers blew up several bars during the 2010 World Cup. Nicole Marrett caught malaria and typhoid on her trip. Observing these kinds of risks, we can't help wondering, "Isn't this foolish?"

THE SAFEST PLACE

Gunmen were holding people up all over the hostel, shouting for wallets and laptops. One of them pressed a gun against Caroline Crawford's chest. Caroline was in Johannesburg, South Africa, with her missionary team. With so many Americans staying at one hotel, it had become a target. Men with guns swarmed the hotel. "I *will* shoot you," they shouted. "Get down now. Get *down*. Over there. NOW!"

One of them pointed the gun at Caroline and said, "Give me your cell phone." She didn't have one and told him so. His reply was chilling, "If you don't have a cell phone, I will kill you."

The gun was pointed at Caroline's head. The man's finger was on the trigger. Caroline thought her death was likely, but then, she had a revelation. When the man threatened her and demanded her cell phone, she said, "I don't have one, so go ahead and kill me." In that moment, she realized she had nothing to fear. She knew her destiny was secure; she had nothing to lose.

The gunman didn't kill her. He turned around and left her alone, but the revelation stayed with her. Caroline had gone to the deepest level of abandonment — a giving up her rights, an abandonment of more than comfort — the right to life itself.

In Luke 9:23, just after the first set of disciples return from their short-term trip, Jesus says, "Whoever wants to be my disciple must deny himself and take up his cross daily and follow me." This is the death we are called to embrace every day — a death to self. This is the kind of abandonment Jesus facilitates in his disciples. The paradox is that this death frees you to really live. And when you've really lived, death loses its sting. That's what enabled Caroline to stand up to the gunman without fear or hesitation.

Death to self sometimes requires us to abandon safety, to leave comfort, to forsake wealth, status, and even relationship. But it also makes possible joy, peace, and love. This death allows us to become fully alive.

Some people say the will of God is the safest place to be. But what about Peter, who was killed by the Romans; crucified upside down, refusing to die the same way as Jesus? What about Paul who was whipped within an inch of his life twice, imprisoned three times, and finally executed? What about *Jesus*?

We are too safe and too comfortable in America. This is why we need to abandon. For the heroes of our faith, it wasn't suffering they were worried might derail them from their destiny, it was safety. Suffering was expected; something they embraced. Our safety keeps us from moving to a place of intimacy. It impoverishes us. Chris McCandless showed us that willful risk-taking can be foolhardy, but most of us are at the other end of the extreme - too comfortable. We need to risk more.

I'd like to suggest that the greatest risk we face these days is that of an unlived life. If we don't question the model of life society gives us, we may one day find ourselves entombed beneath a pyramid of time-payments, mortgages, gadgetry, and playthings. We may wake up one day and see the years have slipped by. We may discover that the dreams of our youth lie caked in dust on the shelves of memory.

God has a lifetime of adventures for you, but they won't happen by accident. You have to make the decision to go. It's up to you to take a chance, to risk security and comfort and leap into the unknown. Life may send a crisis, but when you're trapped by comfort, only *you* can choose to leave.

Thomas Merton says there are seeds of grace flowing from God in every moment. Our only job is to be present enough to receive them. God wants to connect spirit with body. He wants you to understand the kingdom with your five senses. He wants your nerve endings exposed. "Your Kingdom come, your will be done on earth, as it is in heaven," says Jesus (Matthew 6:10). Each moment you experience what God is doing in this life, every time you sense him working in and through you, the kingdom is coming.

CHAPTER 6 NOTES

25. Quoted in BrainyQuote.com, *Andre Gide Quotes,* http://www.brainyquote.com/quotes/authors/a/andre_gide.html.

26. Victor Turner, *The Ritual Process: Structure and Anti-Structure* (Berlin: Aldine De Gruyter, 1969), 95.

27. C.S. Lewis, *The Weight of Glory: And Other Addresses* (New York: HarperCollins Publishers, Inc., 1980), 26.

28. "College Students Have Less Empathy than in Past, Study Shows," *Annals of Psychotherapy & Integrative Health,* http://www.annalsofpsychotherapy.com/articles/news/149/15/College-Students-Have-Less-Empathy-Than-in-Past-Study-Shows.

29. Jean Twenge and W. Keith Campbell, *The Narcissism Epidemic,* 2.

30. Mohan K. Menon and Alex Sharland, "Narcissism, Exploitative Attitudes, and Academic Dishonesty: An Exploratory Investigation of Reality Versus Myth," *Journal of Education for Business,* 86:50-55 (2011), 51.

31. Sterling Hayden, *Wanderer,* (Dobbs Ferry, New York: Sheridan House, 2000), 23-24.

32. Jon Krakauer, *Into the Wild,* (New York: Anchor Books, 1997), 22.

33. Ibid., 199.

CHAPTER 7: BROKENNESS

"If anyone tells you that you can be born again, enlightened, or saved, and go to heaven, and does not first speak to you very honestly about dying, do not believe that person." — Gary Stamper[34]

Karen and I have experienced first-hand the cost of Jesus' lordship. As parents, we knew we could do only so much to help our children understand this. They needed their own kingdom journeys.

After graduating from college in 2007, my son, Seth Jr., left the country to travel the world. Arriving in the Philippines, he volunteered with a local church, mainly doing construction. The three pastors who ran the church lived in a level of poverty that shocked him. One supported his family on five dollars a day. Another had almost no money for food. His family lived off of unripe bananas from the jungle. Even in poverty, they excelled in hospitality. One pastor prepared a feast for Seth and his team that included grilled chicken, fish, and rice: a meal that could have fed the pastor's entire family for four days.

One day, the pastors took Seth to a hospital to pray for an eight-year-old boy named Marvin. Bacterial meningitis had caused the tissues around Marvin's brain to swell. Seizures wracked his body. "I thought this was it … this boy would be healed," said Seth. He put his hand on Marvin's head as seizures went through the boy's body and prayed for healing. This was the moment he would see the miracles Jesus promised. Seth had complete faith.

But nothing happened.

The family ran out of money to pay the doctors. Without money for further treatment, they believed Marvin was as good as dead. Seth and his team came up with enough money ($140 US) for Marvin to receive the treatment. Still, Marvin's condition worsened.

The family sat by the bedside and manually pumped air into the boy's frail lungs. Seth's team helped, but Marvin grew weaker.

The next day, Marvin died.

Seth's team found out that even if Marvin had lived, the swelling of the tissues in his brain would have caused permanent brain damage. His parents came to Seth's team later that day, asking them for $20 to buy wood to build their son a coffin.

My son told me later, "I'd never felt so humbled in my life. I couldn't fathom the thought of constructing my own child's coffin. I couldn't come to grips with a benevolent God that would allow this to happen."

After Marvin's death, Seth Jr. cried out to God in his blog:

> "Lord, I don't know why you do the things
> you do. I don't know why you allow an eight
> year-old boy to die, even after a prayer offered
> in faith. Was there not enough faith? What

more do I need to do to bring your healing power to a suffering eight-year-old?

His mother had to hold his tongue down to keep him from swallowing it. His body was bloated. His brain was damaged. I saw the suffering and I called out to you for healing. I witnessed the pain and tears of his parents. His father's face trembled with the fear of losing his son. And you let it happen."

My son was in a hard place. Marvin's death caused my son to question some of the basic tenets of his faith:

- Is God good?

- Does he want what is best for us?

- Does he continue to work in our lives?

Seth was on a personal pilgrimage, a time to grow in his understanding of God. However, at this point, the journey was putting stress on his relationship with the Lord. We were left wondering, "Is this a good thing?"

JOINING OTHERS IN THEIR BROKENNESS

Mallorie Miller, a college graduate from Ohio, had navigated her kingdom journey for months without having arrived at a place of brokenness. That was before she arrived in Swaziland, a tiny country near the border of South Africa and Mozambique.

Swaziland has the world's highest prevalence of HIV in adults, with 26.3% infected, according to USAID, the U.S.

government's humanitarian assistance agency. Not having the money to buy food, many women in Swaziland become prostitutes — exposing themselves regularly to AIDS. Twelve percent of all children in Swaziland under the age of seventeen have lost one or both parents due to AIDS. One-third of all girls have reported they were sexually assaulted by the time they turned eighteen.

Mallorie, like many new college graduates, dreamed of changing the world. If ever there was a place for dreams to be crushed, Swaziland was it.

Before leaving, Mallorie had been going to graduate school to earn her master's degree in counseling. She was making herself at home in Ashland, Ohio, where she was planning to stay for the next few years. She had a scholarship, an apartment, a great roommate, and a good community. Even though everything looked great, she felt unsatisfied, pursued by the Gift of Restlessness.

Mallorie began to pray and ask friends for advice. As she pressed into prayer, she felt God leading her to take a year off to follow him. Before leaving, she said, "God burdened my heart with a world that needs him. I want to be the hands and feet of Jesus, and I pray that he will pour out his love through me." When she arrived in Swaziland, God began to answer her prayer.

On her way to the hospital in Manzini, Mallorie passed dirt roads lined with shacks made of scavenged wood and tin. Filthy, naked children played in the streets. Women sat barefoot on the ground as they sold shoes and roasted corn over small charcoal stoves.

When Mallorie arrived at the children's ward, a lady in a brown sweater with a baby in her arms made eye contact with her and smiled shyly. RFM Nazarene Hospital is a private missions hospital and significantly better run than the public Swazi hospitals. Still, there were no rooms and the wards were overcrowded. Mallorie walked over to the mother in the brown sweater and sat down.

A few weeks before Swaziland, Mallorie had been in Mozambique. There, she had seen men and women healed miraculously — one of them a young man who had been blind in one eye was healed and could now see with both eyes.

Filled with faith, Mallorie laid her hand on the Swazi baby's head. Then, something strange happened. Mallorie felt her fingers tingle, as if electricity was traveling through her hand. When she pulled her hand away from the baby's forehead, the tingling would stop. Mallorie had intended to spend the morning praying and visiting with other mothers and other children, but instead she stayed with the woman in the brown sweater and her baby. Mallorie wanted to understand this feeling.

Mallorie finally went to visit with some other mothers in the crowded hospital. Suddenly, she heard screaming. Mallorie saw a woman collapse in the hall, wailing in pain. Someone rushed over to help her

Mallorie followed, hoping to see what was going on. Then she saw a baby doubled over on a blanket in an adjoining room. The infant was naked except for a string around its waist. The baby was dead.

"I don't know how to describe it," Mallorie said later, "other than to say that it just felt wrong in my spirit, like such a thing was never intended to exist." Then, she noticed the screaming woman was wearing a brown sweater. It was the same woman she had spent the morning with, and the child lying lifeless on the table was the baby she had prayed for. Mallorie went into shock. "I remember wanting to cry with her. But I couldn't."

The hospital quickly resumed its hurried pace and no one seemed to mind the woman or her pain. Mallorie later learned that eighty percent of the patients who are admitted to the hospital die there. Dead babies, mourning mothers, weeping and wailing: this is the norm at RFM Nazarene hospital.

In the lobby, Mallorie met a man. Two years before, his wife had died at RFM Nazarene hospital. Now, his son was there. "In America, you hear all the beeping machines, and that's how you know when someone dies," he told her. "Here, you just hear screaming."

The hospital kept moving, but Mallorie did not. She sat in the hallway and stared numbly at the floor. The numbness continued into the night. She went to a worship service, but couldn't sing. She hurt too much.

She remembered praying to God, "I know you reign. I know it. I'm just not sure I saw you reign today.'" All that Mallorie could think of was the baby, dead on a hospital table, and the mother weeping on the floor.

Mallorie was broken.

WHY WE NEED BROKENNESS

Michael Hindes talks about how God is like his mother. When he was a kid, she would see his hair sticking up or something amiss, and she would "fuss" with it until it was fixed. Similarly, God won't stop fussing with us if we keep defaulting to a posture of self-reliance to mask our shame. We desperately need to exhaust our personal resources. We need to declare bankruptcy, falling on our knees in dependence on our Lord, who is waiting to be more than a last resort.

We need to arrive at the place where Mallorie found herself — beyond her human limits.

Brokenness is what happens when something *amiss* is exposed and requires change. The change was needed all along; you just didn't realize it. The broken behavior or the broken way of thinking was already in you; it was just not at a place where you saw it in a negative light. Think of all the things that may be broken in us as we grow up. Our narcissism may be just the most obvious of our broken behaviors.

To get to the abundant life Jesus promised, we need to fix what is wrong and incomplete in us. We need to un-break what's broken in our lives. When that happens, we will feel pain. It may even feel like punishment. But it's just God "fussing" over us.

In my life, God has taken away my job, my ability to provide for my family, and my identity. He removed ego props that formed pieces of a false self. Each time, I entered into a time of greater dependence upon him. I was richer for it. Now, I'm grateful.

Brokenness precedes intimacy. People relate to others at their place of greatest brokenness. When we're broken, we are drawn to God. We need him more. He redeems the pain. Once we've come through the brokenness, we can listen with greater obedience. We become people of deeper conviction and more profound compassion who are able to pray for others in the midst of trials.

Mustangs need to be broken before they are able to partner with their rider. On their own, horses are willful and independent. We are not so different from wild horses — God breaks us to help us run faster.

Ruth Wilson experienced this breaking when she started

her kingdom journey in India in 2011. She set up her tent atop an anthill and woke up the next morning with her legs polka-dotted with dozens of inflamed ant bites. "I was in so much pain! A lot of junk bubbled up in my heart," she said. "That week I grew more spiritually than I have ever in my life. God took me down in order to reveal the root of my existence."

When we abandon the things that give us comfort, God brings us to brokenness, which allows us to unpack the baggage others have saddled on us. We begin to discover our true self. Brokenness finishes abandonment's job; it strips away the false self. It allows God to transform us into a new creation.

Many people are offended by brokenness. "God wants to bless, not curse us," they say. "He wants us to be joyful, not despairing. If you're doing the Christian life right, then you should be happy and faith-filled. If you are hurt and full of doubt, then you are doing something wrong." Unfortunately, this is not how God works, but it's often how we think.

After experiencing abandonment, the things that used to help you buffer pain are gone. In that space, anything can happen. That's why brokenness is the second stage of a kingdom journey. Life doesn't work like we think it's supposed to work.

Seth's failure to heal Marvin in the midst of his confident faith made him question what he knew about God. Similarly, Mallorie struggled to reconcile a child's death with her understanding of a God completely in control. Something needed to change. Something needed to be resolved. Had they lost their faith? Should they have quit and enrolled in a theology class until they better understood God's nature? No, they were in exactly the right place — moving on their kingdom journeys to experience brokenness. They'd had a good education; it just wasn't complete.

God is bigger than the boxes we've put him in. Before we can get a new understanding, God has to deconstruct our old one. Through the centuries, believers have noticed how important brokenness is to becoming the person God intended us to be. Some call this the "dark night of the soul" or a "wilderness experience." Whatever we call it, we know from experience that sometimes a little breaking and excavating has to happen before a solid foundation can be built. Questioning is healthy; maybe even necessary.

George Barna, researcher and founder of The Barna Group, writes in his book *Maximum Faith* about the ten stages in our faith walk. The seventh and hardest stage is brokenness. It is also the most important.

Barna says we need to be broken in three main areas: sin, self, and society. According to Barna, American culture is one of the biggest barriers to brokenness. In the United States, we value comfort, security, and confidence, which impede brokenness. Barna so highly emphasizes brokenness that he says biblical brokenness is meant to happen before someone becomes "born again."[35]

The irony of our culture is that we do everything in our power to avoid it — brokenness.

Seth's and Mallorie's concepts of God were too small. At first, Seth felt like a bad Christian; he doubted what he once believed. Once he went through the experience, he could see why it was necessary. The old ways didn't work — they were broken. His ideals didn't match up with reality. He had been broken, but oblivious to the fact. He thought to himself, "I don't know what to believe anymore."

Seth learned an important lesson: if we are to be transformed, we need to first be broken. Brokenness clears away the obstacles that get in the way of transformation.

FEELING INADEQUATE

Even on a kingdom journey, people find ways to escape.

My son-in-law, Joe, and his ministry team were stuck waiting for a bus in downtown Eldoret, Kenya. A few street kids came up and asked for money. His teammate, Matt, decided to buy the kids bread. Lauren, another teammate, started making friends with them. She scolded them about sniffing glue. She took away their bottles, emptying their pockets for the hidden extras. Danielle, a nurse, cleaned some of their cuts with a first-aid kit she had in her backpack.

All the while, Joe did nothing.

He tried talking to a few of them and eventually lost patience. He didn't have any medical skills like Danielle or the charisma of Lauren. He thought about giving money or food, but he wasn't sure what to do. "Wouldn't that make them more dependent on us?" Joe wondered. "Why are there so many dirty, glue-sniffing kids, anyway?"

Joe watched as hundreds of Kenyans walked by, not doing anything. He felt inadequate and ashamed. After a while, as his friends ministered to the street kids, he realized he *did* have something to offer. Joe had journalism experience. He wondered if he could investigate and see what was being done for the street kids. But before he could do anything, the bus arrived.

Back at the mission base, Joe pondered whether it would be too much trouble to pursue his idea. He remembered how difficult it was to be in the city with dozens of dirty street kids around him. It was exhausting and chaotic. Did he really want to go through all that his idea would require?

I teach those who go on kingdom journey the importance

of pressing into pain. If you feel uncomfortable, then probably something good is happening. When we lose focus and run from pain, we miss our chance to grow. It's natural to want to retreat to the isolation of our false self. This is why it is so important to go on a journey with a community of trusted people to hold you accountable. They can call you out when you get cranky or act out in frustration.

Joe avoided thinking about it for a few days. Finally, he sat down and prayed, "God, do you want me to do this or not?" His chest grew warm and his head started buzzing with ideas. By the time he got up, he had made his decision. Joe asked his friends, Lauren and Matt, to help him. Joe began going to the street every day to build relationships. He hired a translator named Moses to help communicate with the kids.

One day, the team met a man named Joseph who ran a center that offered classes and a safe environment to area children. Joseph offered insight into how to minister to the street kids. Moses also took them to an orphanage that took care of former street kids. The environment there was terrible.

In the orphanage, there were thirty-four children crammed into two rooms the size of one small bedroom. The caretakers also ran a school for sixty-two children, packing half of them into one of the rooms while the other half were taught outside. The orphanage was in an apartment complex. There was a well in the center filled with unclean drinking water, which caused many of the children to contract dysentery.

Joe watched as a three-year-old orphan urinated into a puddle around the well. Wanting to help, Joe decided he would try raising money to prevent orphans from going to the streets in the first place.

Joe began talking to the pastors who ran the orphanage about funding a new building for them. But Joe's local contact had a bad feeling about it and wanted to make sure the money would go to the right place. They investigated the orphanage. It turned out that Joe's contact was right; the pastors were lying. The "orphanage" only appeared to exist.

Joe and his team were crushed as they learned that children were rounded up from the neighboring slum and passed-off as orphans. They felt betrayed.

Sometimes you enter brokenness through a shattered dream. Joe's good intentions were not enough. In the middle of his disillusionment, he felt God's hand over him. "We were really upset," Joe said, "but you know what? I don't regret getting involved. Everyone who does work like this has battle scars. Everyone has stories of betrayal and hurt. They are learning experiences, and you need them in order to do the really great things. I'm just glad that I took a chance. Even though we were going down a dead end, I felt so alive those two weeks."

In the end, the pain is worth it. Brokenness is a part of life. When we embrace it, we can learn from it. We can find healing and move on. "When I am weak, he is strong," is how Paul puts it. When we are authentically our broken selves, God's image shines brightest through us.

BROKENNESS VISITS US IN CYCLES

We practice brokenness — this discipline of emptying ourselves — so that we can be filled with God's life. The same things we experience on our journeys happen in real life — over and over again. You won't be broken once. You will be broken again and again and again. You won't have to surrender once. You'll have to surrender and surrender and surrender.

When you get home from your journey, you may expect everyone to be interested in what you experienced. When they're not, you have yet another chance to empty yourself. When life comes at you with all its monotony, you get to break again. One day, when you lay down to die, you empty yourself a final time.

This is what Jesus was talking about when he said we must each carry our own cross daily. We are never rid of pain. The quality of living may have greatly improved over the centuries for many cultures, but life is still hard. Kingdom journeys not only give us the raw material of pain, they give us the tools to process pain. By leading us to brokenness, they lead us to God.

The alternative is to run. You can take a pill to make your pain go away. You can watch a movie. You can drink a beer or go to sleep. You can eat your banana muffin and your pint of ice cream. Those things will push away the pain ... for a while.

But pain, like an infected wound, tends to grow worse with time. God designed it as a signal; a flashing light telling us something is wrong. It's better to go through the pain with God. Give it to him. Talk about it with him. Explore where it came from and why God allowed it in your life.

We go on a journey not only to illuminate our broken places, but also to learn to deal with future brokenness. We remember what it felt like before. We feel the glory of freedom and weigh it against the dull throb of living with hidden pain. We come to understand the logic of the process: we have to be broken ... so we can be filled.

If it ever seems as if I have my act totally together, I invite you to read my journals. This particular book may be in your hands, but over the years I have regularly been turned down for book deals. Editors look at my writing and they see flaws. At work, I'm daily reminded of where others are more talented than me. In my home, I periodically bump up against my broken behavior. I'm as broken as anyone.

The same is true for my family. Two of my children have struggled with depression. One has hugely frustrating handicaps that make every day a challenge. Most days if I were called upon to write a family Christmas letter, it wouldn't sound pretty. Yet, all along God has had me right where he wanted me. I live reminded of my need for his grace because I'm broken without him.

Brokenness is a reality check. It tells me, "You're not really in control here. In fact, you need more help than you realize." God uses failure to bring us to brokenness, to force us back to a posture of dependence. He uses brokenness to teach us thankfulness for small blessings and to teach us humility that makes us more accessible to others. As a result, we become more approachable, even more loveable.

Brokenness strips away pretense and leads us along the difficult path to self-knowledge, a rare gift in this age of distraction. Self-knowledge then drives us back to a place of dependence on God. And we begin again.

The cycle of brokenness must continue even after a kingdom journey. We need the gut-check if we are to rediscover the goodness of Christ. After we first visit brokenness on a journey, it's a place God causes us to revisit for the rest of our lives. God never wants us to stop growing in our love and dependence on him.

CHAPTER 7 NOTES

34. Gary Stamper, "Men are Hurting," *The Integral Warrior,* http://www.garystamper.blogspot.com/2010/05/men-are-hurting.html.

35. Barna Group, "Research on How God Transforms Lives Reveals a 10-Stop Journey," *Barna Group: Examine. Illuminate. Transform,* http://www.barna.org/transformation-articles/480-research-on-how-god-transforms-lives-reveals-a-10-stop-journey.

CHAPTER 8: BROKENNESS & SURRENDER

"Never surrender opportunity for security." — Branch Rickey[36]

In 1987, I took our whole family on a kingdom journey of sorts. Most people call the U-Haul process "moving." Done well, it can begin to look and feel like a kingdom journey. You pack the truck, say goodbye to friends and all that's familiar; then you leave home. You hope for a better life ahead and join a new community where you arrive as a stranger.

I had graduated from business school in Virginia and accepted a job in Florida. Now Karen and I were pursuing a call to ministry — it was both scary and exhilarating.

Two years later, the journey entered a dark phase after I was fired. We were slowly coming to realize what it meant to have five children under the age of seven. An avalanche of toys, diapers, and baby paraphernalia filled our home and even spilled out onto the driveway. We put our heads down and began to gut it out.

I started a new ministry and two or three side businesses. I managed them all out of a ramshackle office I'd built in our garage. As cramped as this was, it was still an improvement from the dining room table where I had begun several months earlier.

That whole year was a scramble to survive, beginning with the ignominy of losing a steady job. Without insurance, Karen and I turned to Medicaid to help cover her last pregnancy. We were scrambling, all right — for dignity and identity, as well as for cash flow. My mind was filled with thoughts like, "If the sacrificial investment I'd made to launch the ministry meant so little, what good was I?" And, "What can I ever really count on?"

We hunkered down — Karen with the babies and me with my ragged half-formed ideas for keeping the wolves from the door. It was a time for grieving, but there was no time for grief. So if we felt broken, we stayed focused. Even in firefighting mode, I was waking up to the needs of our children. How would we bring them up to cope with all that life would throw at them?

Somewhere in that desperate place, I cried out to God. All I seemed to get in response was silence. It confirmed what I'd always suspected, but was only coming to believe: we Christians could advertise a "personal relationship with Jesus Christ" until we were blue in the face, but whatever relationship I had with God was decidedly impersonal.

What kind of friend doesn't respond when you call on them? Is this what God expected of me? Is this what I would pass along to my children? How would they subsist on the watery gruel of academic Bible studies on which I'd been weaned? In my spiritually shell-shocked condition, it wasn't working. I didn't have much faith the next year would be any different. I was desperate for change.

Survival seemed an ambitious goal. "If we can just get through another year," Karen and I would say to each other. When I could look down the road, the outlook for anything *more* than a standard-issue American spirituality for my children seemed bleak. It left me asking God for answers, not for me, but for them. How would we help them experience a feast of faith that we hadn't even tasted? During those years, a relationship with God seemed like a cruel, cosmic joke.

I had hit the brokenness stage, been spun around, and spanked hard by a series of circumstances that left me sputtering like someone who's been dunked under the water too long. God and life seemed to demand, "Say 'Uncle!'"

I'd had enough.

I had long since surrendered. I was waving the white flag and shouting "UNCLE!" It felt like each new day I was freshly humbled. I learned to embrace every opportunity to turn whining into prayer.

At some point, I guess my "Oh, God! Help!" prayers reached critical mass in the ears of the Almighty, because I got an answer. Only, it didn't look like hope. Rather, it came dressed in the form of a crisis that made my knees buckle. I felt so bad I could do nothing but cry out in desperation.

I was a hard case. I resisted brokenness, holding out as long as I could. At that point in my life, I had ego props that allowed me to coast along pretty well in self-sufficient mode. I had a model marriage, a beautiful family, and a reputation for integrity. But through a series of painful events, life's rug was pulled out from under me. At a marriage retreat in Titusville, Florida, I broke.

For the first time in my life, I heard the Lord's voice. *He told me that he loved me.* That was all I needed to know. It was enough to keep going.

On the other side of the pain, I found what I had been looking for the whole time: a real relationship with my Creator. Yes, it about killed me to get there. Once I surrendered, God welcomed me like a prodigal son and began to speak to me in a way that I had never experienced. Surrender was tough, but what came next was worth it. I started to see every challenging situation not as an insurmountable obstacle I had to tough out, but as a chance to demonstrate faith. In short, I started to ask God for help.

You might ask, "Is all that pain and suffering necessary? Can't we just surrender early in the process?" I've got to say, if you can do it, early surrender is the best strategy. "Just trust God and you'll be okay," right? But if you're as addicted to control as I was, how do you give up your rights? Often, the journey has to take you to a point where surrender feels like the only option.

The good news is that God is patient. He'll move us slowly, allowing us to give up control over time. Or we can get out of the way by hoisting the white flag and welcome immediate change. It's up to us. But it helps to realize God is going to take us to the point of surrender at a pace we can handle.

There's life on the other side of the disaster. It's sweet. Knowing that, it's worth pondering, "Why not give him what he wants?"

ENDURING YOUR SEASON OF PAIN

Even on a kingdom journey, you can find ways to escape pain instead of pressing into it. The stronger your will, the more difficult it may be to accept the lessons brokenness can teach you. How do we willingly surrender to brokenness?

A few weeks after sleeping on an anthill, world traveler, Ruth Wilson, was sick and bedridden in Nepal. Her team was working with a church high in the Himalayan Mountains. Ruth was sick for a week. After her fever broke, she set out with her team, following a Nepalese pastor up steep mountains.

A quarter of the way up a mountain, Ruth realized she had a problem. During her sickness, her muscles had atrophied. The high altitude and steep grades exhausted her to the point of her breaking. Ruth's lungs burned and she didn't think she could make it to the top.

Ruth was about to give up when she heard God whisper in her spirit, "Just put one foot in front of the other, but don't look up." She knew if she looked up and saw the huge mountain above her she would have quit. Instead, she kept her head down, and took one small step at a time. After what felt like an eternity, she reached the top of the mountain and was able to enjoy the beautiful, green vista below. If the hike had been a death march, this was her *Sound of Music* moment.

Ruth began applying what she'd learned on that mountain to the rest of her journey. Some days, she wanted to quit. She knew God had called her, but there were times when everything was too hard and too uncomfortable. The hike required vulnerability that continually stretched her to a breaking point. "When I feel like that," she said, "I just hear him say, 'One foot in front of the other.'"

Ruth learned that surrender involves trusting God in the midst of pain, recognizing that he doesn't always want us to be comfortable. He has an end goal in mind. God's not sadistic, but the freedom he wants for us comes with a price. His plan is to see us become fully alive. He knows the way to get there is the same wilderness road Jesus and the disciples took.

The bad habits and self-sufficient ways we adopt become so natural — they become invisible chains that restrict our spiritual movement. We don't even see the bondage we're in. Prying our chains loose will usually hurt. It may feel like suffering.

Holy suffering may come to us in a variety of disguises or as naked and throbbing as a migraine headache. Given that, should we go out looking for opportunities to suffer? No — we don't have to. The reality is that suffering on a kingdom journey, as in life, will always find us. Instead of looking for suffering, we search for the kingdom.

"Seek first the kingdom of God," counsels Jesus (Matthew 6:33). Of course the kingdom is full of broken people. Locating our own brokenness is part of the price of admission. We just need to be ready for it when it comes, without fear, knowing it has a purpose as an important part of our journey.

BE A VICTIM OR SURRENDER

Pain compels us to change — it's hard to stay broken. God's plan has always been to lead us first into brokenness and then to dependence as we surrender to him. When you get to brokenness you have two options: 1) become a victim and effectively numb your soul, or 2) surrender, allowing God to transform you. It's a crossroads. "Die or be killed," as my friend Andrew Shearman says.

Recently, a Christian author was attacked for his views. He responded by saying, "We all have a choice when we are spoken of in negative terms. You can throw rocks back and become equally mean and nasty, or you can allow that pain to shape you into the kind of person who loves their enemies and who is more open and more expansive and more humble. It shapes you. It shapes you one way or the other; there is no third place. You either become equally bitter and fearful and angry and mean — or the pain pushes you into this place where you're broken, and because you're broken, God can fill you in new ways."[37]

The weekend after Marvin, the young Filipino boy, died, Seth Jr. hiked through the Philippine mountains on a trail that passed seven waterfalls. Even though the views were spectacular, the weather pleasant, and the waterfalls refreshing, he felt haunted by the Marvin's memory. He felt like God had let him down. The healing he'd pleaded with God for never came and Seth was left to wonder just how much he could trust God.

When he saw hundreds of gallons of river pouring over the seventh and last waterfall, Seth felt his spirit surge. His heart began to beat a little faster. Something inside whispered that he needed to stand under the crushing flow. So, he threw off his shirt and jumped in.

"When I made it to the place where the water fell," Seth wrote on his blog afterward, "I threw my arms upward and stepped under it. The weight of the water falling over me was too great for me to stand beneath and it pummeled me." Eventually, he bobbed to the surface and swam toward the waterfall again. Again, he stood underneath it. Again he was pushed down.

As Seth's body went underneath the cascading river, he felt an emotional release. It was as if his burdens were being washed off him in the rushing water. "Each time I bobbed up, a weight was taken off until it was gone." Through the experience, he felt God whispering words of peace to his heart:

Seth, it's okay.
Seth, you are going to die, too, someday.
Seth, I've got this.
Seth, I am so much greater than you could
ever imagine and I am infinitely greater than
your perception of me right now.

Later, Seth confessed, "Some piece of me died on the mountain that day and I came out more stable in my faith in God than I'd ever been. I didn't understand the *why* of it all, but I knew deep in the core of my being that it didn't matter. God would still be God in the fullness of his character."

I love the way my son physically surrendered to God. He placed himself under a waterfall, allowing it to crush him. Each time he went under — in a sort of baptism — he was inviting God to break him, to take away his control, to throw him down. He kept going back for more until the process was complete. This is what surrender looks like. It's saying to God, "I don't care how bad it hurts. If you're in it, I want it. I choose you."

Brokenness is a critical stage on the journey, but it's not the end. The question is will you allow the brokenness to transform your faith or will you run?

Surrender may take you to a new level of leaning upon God. You have to get to a point where you say "yes" to his questions, whatever they are. You have to believe he has your absolute best in mind. You have to know you can trust him.

When I occasionally go through a hard season and feel estranged from myself, I remind myself to look beyond my own little world. I ask, "Have I surrendered? Am I listening for God's voice?" Oftentimes, quieting my anxious heart and distracted mind are the first steps to getting through brokenness one more time.

NOT SURRENDERING

Jesus was uncompromising in what he asked of his followers: complete surrender. Read what he says about a narrow road and taking up your cross and you'll find little wiggle room. He was a radical and asks us to be radicals, too. We can ignore his words or disobey them, but if we're serious followers, we'll pay attention.

There is also a cost to *not* surrendering. What if you're fighting for the wrong thing? What if you insist on calling the shots instead of submitting? What if you're clinging to something you'd be better off without?

When we don't surrender, we're faced with an unpleasant reality: that we may be hypocrites. We proclaim that Jesus is Lord and that he gets to call the shots in our life; however, we stubbornly still cling to our own rights and expectations.

The cost of not surrendering is that you'll settle for a cheap substitute, never embracing God's best. The apostle Paul describes it as "having a form of godliness but denying its power," (2 Timothy 3:5). The cost of not surrendering is that you'll continue on in bondage while claiming to be free. Persist in it and eventually you will begin to define yourself in terms of what you *can't* do. You may even become cynical.

The paradox is this: We were made to be free, but we must give up our freedom to get there. We must make a counterintuitive transaction: give our lives away to get them back. As Bob Dylan sang, "You've got to serve somebody."[38] So, the question is not, "Will I surrender?" but, "To whom will I surrender? Who will I serve?" When we choose to not trust God, we're really just choosing to trust only ourselves.

Surrender is, in a way, optional. You can drag out the miserable process for years or you can choose to end it today. Many people try to avoid surrender. They develop mechanisms to delay their personal day of reckoning.

You can keep backing up, keep postponing, but eventually you will be forced to choose liberty or death. On that day, you'll be stuck between irony and paradox. Jesus wants to set you free, but you are going to have to die to yourself first. If you don't, you are effectively choosing self — the essence of spiritual bondage and death.

Of course, choosing not to surrender will keep you in a state of brokenness indefinitely. Oddly enough, for some people, this beats giving up control. In their broken minds, it's better than saying "yes" to an uncertainty, better than having to trust. Some people spend their lives staving off the decision to surrender.

Surrender may feel optional. It is also inevitable. Everyone surrenders. You eventually surrender to death. Before you die, you may have to yield to the forces of disease, divorce, or depression. We all raise the white flag at some point. Given that inevitability, I have to ask, why not gamble a bit and trust God?

In 1974, Lieutenant Hiroo Onoda finally stopped fighting World War II. Onoda had been conducting guerilla operations in the Philippines for over thirty years. For three decades he had set fire to farms, attacked Philippine villagers, and engaged in numerous firefights with the authorities. When he finally laid down his arms, Onoda was the last Japanese officer to surrender. It came twenty-nine years after Japan's original surrender to the allies. Why did it take so long?

In 1944, Onoda was ordered by Major Taniguchi to Lubang Island, a tiny island in the Philippines. His orders stated explicitly that he was not to surrender. When the Allies attacked the island in 1945, all but three of Onoda's comrades surrendered or were killed. He did not, at least, not for another twenty-nine years. (Sound like anyone you know?)

July 26, 1945, the Potsdam Declaration was delivered to the Japanese Emperor and government. "We call upon the government of Japan," the declaration states, "to proclaim now the unconditional surrender of all Japanese armed forces. The alternative for Japan is prompt and utter destruction." These last lines are chilling, considering that an atomic bomb was being loaded onto a plane 1500 miles away.

Several months prior to this, the military junta that formed the Japanese government stated that Japan would fight to extinction rather than surrender. If the Japanese had known what was going to happen to Hiroshima and Nagasaki four days after they rejected the terms of the Potsdam Declaration, would they have surrendered?

Even after the Allies' two atomic bombs annihilated over 150,000 Japanese citizens, the government still struggled to surrender. It was almost a fifty-fifty split between those officials who wanted to continue the fight to extinction and those who were willing to give up.

When it became clear Emperor Shōwa would surrender, some of the top army officers led a coup to stop him. They ended up occupying the royal palace for several hours before they were stopped and forced to abandon their rebellion. In the months after the war, many Japanese soldiers, including top generals, committed suicide because they were so ashamed of their surrender.[39]

All these years later, the Japanese army looks fanatical. But how strange is their behavior really? In many ways, we are all like those men… unwilling to give up, to admit defeat and humbly submit to someone else — even to God.

WHY IS SURRENDER SO DIFFICULT?

The point of kingdom journey is to learn to live a free life, one where you partner with God to achieve his dream for planet earth. But for Jesus to be our Lord, the issue of control has to come up. If we believe we are fully self-sufficient, we will never surrender.

A few months after the signing of the Instrument of Surrender, Japanese planes dropped thousands of leaflets declaring surrender on Lubang Island. Every time Lieutenant Onoda was ordered to surrender, he refused. He believed it was a hoax concocted by the Allies to trick him into giving up his mission. Finally, in the 1970s, Onoda's superior officer, Major Taniguchi, was found. He was flown to the island and ordered Onoda to surrender.

Finally, Lieutenant Onoda laid down his arms. Onoda had killed thirty Filipinos during that time; however, his strange circumstances led the president of the Philippines to give him a full pardon. Onoda returned home to Japan where he wrote a book about his experiences entitled *No Surrender*.[40]

Surrender is never fun. Usually, it's humiliating. Think about Emperor Shōwa surrendering after two atomic bombs or Hiroo Onoda. What did surrender mean for them? Look at what the Japanese were asked to give up when they surrendered to the Allies:

- Their **control**

- Their **lifestyle**

- Their **rights**

- Their **comfort**

- Their **pride**

- Their **self-righteousness**

They gave up a way of life. Customs would change. Laws would change. Economic systems would change. Viewed from our privileged vantage point, we can claim, "Yeah, they changed for the better." But at the time, who knew? They were entering into the unknown. The future was far from certain. As R.E.M. sings, it was, "the end of the world as we know it."[41]

Knowing surrender is so important, how does God get us to a point where we are willing to do it? Often, the cost of surrender is so high we don't consider it unless we have to. For the Japanese, it took two atomic bombs and the threat of a third. Honestly, how different are we?

Of all the reasons God sends us on a kingdom journey, this is one of the most important: to teach us to surrender. It's the fruit of brokenness. General William Booth, founder of the Salvation Army said, "The greatness of a man's power is the measure of his surrender."[42]

What have you had to surrender? Take inventory. Have you surrendered your home, your car, your lifestyle, your dreams, and your friendships?

THE CONSEQUENCES OF NOT SURRENDERING

Even from a distance, you can tell the people who haven't surrendered. You'll see a number of telltale signs:

- Chaos follows their personal lives

- They play the victim card

- They struggle to maintain control

- They get their feelings hurt and hurt other people's feelings

- They tend to make the same mistakes repeatedly

- Life tends to revolve around their needs

If you give Lordship lip service, your life may look like that, too. We want the benefits of his Lordship without the costs. We want him to protect, guide, and comfort us, but are we prepared to surrender?

The irony is that when things go wrong, we rail against God and blame him. In this modern era, we struggle with the concept of Lordship. We don't really have much experience with authority. We treasure independence and democracy, but fail to appreciate the importance of submission.

Eventually we must recognize that God is the Lord of his creation. Eventually we stop operating under the illusion of self-sufficiency.

God won't fully use us until we take a knee.

CHAPTER 8 NOTES

36. Quoted in BrainyQuote.com, *Branch Rickey Quotes*, http://www.brainyquote.com/quotes/authors/b/branch_rickey.html.

37. Quoted in Josh Lujan Loveless, "Is Rob Bell a Universalist," *Relevant: God. Life. Progressive Culture.*, http://www.relevantmagazine.com/god/church/features/25030-is-rob-bell-a-universalist.

38. Bob Dylan, "Gotta Serve Somebody" in *Slow Train Coming* (New York: Columbia Records, 1979).

39. Hiroo Onoda, *No Surrender: My Thirty-Year War*, (Annapolis, MD: Naval Institute Press, 1999).

40. Ibid.

41. Michael Stipe, "It's the End of the World as We Know It (And I feel Fine)," single, (Hollywood, CA: I.R.S. Records, 1987).

42. Quoted in ThinkExist.com, *William Booth Quotes*, http://thinkexist.com/quotes/william_booth/.

CHAPTER 9: GETTING THROUGH BROKENNESS

"To dare is to lose one's footing momentarily. To not dare is to lose oneself." — Soren Kierkegaard[43]

Some people are broken, but haven't embraced brokenness. Many followers of Jesus have stopped at the gate to the narrow road, unwilling to go farther on the journey. Jesus asks them for surrender, but they prefer to call their own shots.

The bad news about getting to brokenness is you are likely to experience a profound sense of disorientation. What used to come naturally, no longer works. You're unsure of yourself. As you look at the parts of your life that feel hopelessly broken, it's easy to conclude, "I'm a mess. I'm useless to anybody. I should just give up."

The truth is you were always a mess, always broken. Just like the rest of us. Getting to brokenness involves coming to a greater awareness of what others can plainly see. Many go blithely through life, ignorant of the things that sabotage their relationships and jobs. Eventually, God will allow the evidence of your brokenness to accumulate until it reaches a tipping point. Then, you will have to acknowledge that what you're doing isn't working and that you need to make a change.

Walking through brokenness is important, but it is still not enough to transform us. We can go to the most remote places on earth and if we don't press into the pain and discomfort, we will walk away unchanged. We have to let brokenness complete its work in us. In that regard, Christie Albaugh gives us a good example.

THE MELTDOWN

A few years ago, Christie was on a journey in Cambodia, climbing mountains, and volunteering at an orphanage, teaching English. One hot, rainy night she was on her way home and walked into "a horde of insects." Hundreds of bugs swarmed around a light bulb in the hallway and blocked her way to her room. Even the floor of the hallway was covered with them. She would have to step on and squish the bugs to get into her room. To make matters worse, the bugs started to dive-bomb her face, catching in her hair.

Christie decided it was now or never; she would make a break for the door. She raised her shirt collar in front of her nose and dashed for the door. Once in her room, she took a deep breath of relief until she quickly realized she had another problem — she had to go to the bathroom.

The squatty potty was outside, and Christie wasn't about to brave "the horde" again. So she decided to ignore her bladder and go to bed, although it was only 8:30 p.m.

Christie's bed was a sleeping bag on top of a thin camping pad, A pink mosquito net covered it all. As she cleared away the dead bugs that had fallen around her bed, her foot slid into a puddle of water. The roof had leaked onto her bed and it was soaked. That's when she finally lost it.

At this point, Christie had been traveling for two months in her year-long journey. The accumulated aggravations finally boiled over. She began to scream in frustration.

"I feel gross and I can't shower!" she howled. "My hair has bugs in it. I can't leave the room. It's raining outside, so it's going to be muddy tomorrow. The room is a disaster. I can't be alone. It's hot, and I'm sweating. I have to practically sit on the ground to pee. For the past seven days all I've eaten is rice. My legs are hairy. My team doesn't understand me. The bugs and water are attacking my bed. I have to shower with a bucket. I haven't stopped sweating since I left California. I can't go running here. We can only access the Internet once a week. I can't walk through the room without ducking through four different laundry lines. And it has been over a week since I've eaten any chocolate!"

> **THE TRUTH IS YOU WERE ALWAYS A MESS, ALWAYS BROKEN. JUST LIKE THE REST OF US. GETTING TO BROKENNESS INVOLVES COMING TO A GREATER AWARENESS OF WHAT OTHERS CAN PLAINLY SEE.**

Her explosion lasted about fifteen minutes.

None of it surprised God. The truth is, we all come to breaking point like this in our journeys. If we are pressing into the pain and God is challenging us, it's unavoidable. This is the moment God waits for, when everything falls apart, when all that we've been suppressing finally erupts.

God is not offended by little tirades like Christie's. He'd probably have been more disappointed had she prayed a nice prayer like, "God, you're so great," while seething inside. He always prefers our honest doubts, fears, and frustrations to hypocritical piety.

Arriving at this breaking point is essential if we are to move beyond brokenness. We have a choice to press in or opt out. As a parent of five, I know that battles over control are inevitable. Children want their own way, even when it isn't the best for them.

What Christie wanted was comfort, and she was willing to scream and pout to get it. She had come to her breaking point. It's interesting that after she completed her kingdom journey, Christie, of all people, went on to serve for over a year at an orphanage in the Philippines. There, she lived in a rat-infested apartment and dealt with the heat and insects of the tropics year-round.

During the months between her breakdown and return to the Philippines, Christie matured. "I know I was never promised comfort," she said. "I know it's good for me to not always be comfortable." God transformed her from being addicted to comfort to someone who could be content without it.

Christie desperately needed to exhaust her personal resources and declare bankruptcy. Like Christie, the rest of us need to get to the end of ourselves, too. The catch is, we can't get there until we are willing to be authentic. Our words may not sound pious or pretty, they just need to come from the heart.

BROKENNESS IN COMMUNITY

It was a beautiful day on the beach. Daniel Stinson and his mission team had been traveling in some of the most scenic parts of the world for three months: New Zealand, Australia, and the Philippines.

The forty people in Daniel's team had become family to him. They did everything together — eat, work, play, and pray. His team was his community, his mobile church. One of their last days in the Philippines, Daniel's team traveled to one of the country's most beautiful beaches. They loved its white sands and crystal clear waters.

But the serenity of the beach masked a lack of cohesion in the group. If you could have looked beneath the surface in the month prior, you'd have seen that the team's relationships had ebbed into shallow. They lived together, but they didn't know each other. Physically, they shared close quarters, but they had isolated themselves emotionally and spiritually. They were living the words of Death Cab for Cutie's song, "Like brothers on a hotel bed." They were near each other, but not really connecting. Many felt bitter pangs of loneliness in the midst of the crowd.

While Daniel and his team enjoyed the beach, one of his teammates, Mike, sat down on a towel. Daniel didn't notice his pained expression. A personal trainer, Mike was fit, but during the previous week he had been laid low with a bout of kidney stones. For most of the afternoon, Mike sat on the beach in pain, while Daniel and the rest of the group swam, played Frisbee, and enjoyed the warm weather.

"I walked by him several times," Daniel admitted. "I never prayed for him. I never asked if there was anything I could do for him."

When the sun began to set over the Pacific, the group started to pack up to go home. Daniel was carrying a cooler back to the bus when one of his teammates asked him to join in praying for Mike, who was still lying on the beach in pain.

As the two of them walked over to pray, the rest of the group also surrounded Mike. When Daniel prayed, he believed God was going to bring complete healing to Mike. Despite his confidence, Mike wasn't healed. Daniel broke off from the group feeling upset and confused. "Why won't you heal Mike?" he asked God. "Do you see how much pain he is in?" Then, he sensed God's reply: "I will, but not yet. Trust that I am good."

Daniel returned to the group, which was still praying. He noticed that something had changed in the dynamic. A spirit of repentance broke out in the group. People began confessing that they had been selfish, insincere, and prideful.

The community had not treated one another well over the month before. Convicted, individuals went to each other and apologized. Daniel repented to the group and to God of his own selfishness. He later reported that, God "enlarged my heart to love my team for the very first time."

The team continued to pray for Mike, believing he would be healed. Together, they helped him back on the bus. Two hours later, he was pain-free.

There is something about the healing power of a community that humbles itself and prays together.

Daniel's group had embarked on a kingdom journey together and had been with each other for three months. They abandoned their old lives, but didn't give up the old routine of self-reliance. Soon, they slouched into independence, numbing themselves to their own pain and the pain of the people around them. They became distracted.

Thinking they were going to have a fun day at the beach, they couldn't see how their community had become shallow and insincere, their community broken.

What did God do? He allowed the strongest and most self-reliant of them to become physically broken so they would be forced to confront their own self-reliance. Their weakness surprised them. God broke one to break them all and their brokenness became an important healing part of the journey.

FEAR OF BROKENNESS

People are afraid of brokenness. It hurts. It can feel claustrophobic. Some feel they won't be able to endure the pain. Who but a masochist likes pain? We naturally seek comfort, security, safety, and peace. The problem is this: to heal us, God wants to expose our brokenness. The narrow path to peace is often through the fields of pain.

If you want to go on a kingdom journey, you will often be asked to pick up your cross and carry it. Some days your knees will buckle under its weight. *The cross is your weakness.* There are aspects of your life that just don't work, and parts of yourself that you would prefer no one would ever see. Jesus calls us to pick up our brokenness and carry it. He calls us to embrace it.

What happens when we try to run from brokenness? What happens when we try to stay in a place of dysfunctional comfort? Spiritual progress stops. Everything may appear okay on the outside, but inside we become numb — slowly dying.

Kingdom journey is such an effective discipline as it forces us to focus on the present. It calls our attention to the broken places within us by taking us to places of pain far from our comfort zones. If the journey is too short, we may be able to avoid dealing with brokenness. Anyone can hold his or her breath under water for a short time. But a good kingdom journey will lead through the raw brokenness to a place of greater faith and dependence. Community makes that part of the journey so much easier.

SHAME AS A BARRIER

Shame is one of the primary obstacles of our processing brokenness. We can't change until we confront it and finish the job. When we are in shame, we are afraid that there is something wrong with us, that if someone found out about it, they would exclude us. Shame attacks our basic identity as a person.

Shame causes us to withdraw both from God and other people — it throws up roadblocks to deep meaningful relationships. It causes us to use masks and hide the parts of ourselves we don't like.

To avoid shame, we create a false self. The false self is the mask we put on, the applause-seeking performance to get the connection we crave. Our false self is funnier, more interesting, more socially adept, sweeter, bolder, more athletic, wealthier, and more confident than our truest selves.

Starved for connection, some people will even use their false self to get negative attention. They create a false persona that is more rebellious, angrier, more insulting, and more violent than true. The false self is more — it's more than you, but in the end, it's not you at all. It isn't real in the sense that it's not who God created you to be. By definition, it is false —

a counterfeit of the real thing.

The false self shows up in the flaw-free image we attempt to project. Our homes and cars look good. Our Christmas cards proclaim our achievements. When asked, "How are you?" We say, "Great!" But the reality is that life is hard. There just aren't many places for people to talk about it.

Authenticity and vulnerability are the antidotes to shame and the fear of disconnection. Shame shuts down connection with others. Not only can you not receive love when you are in shame, you can't give it either. The good news is that vulnerability allows us to move from shame to empathy.

While on her kingdom journey, Ruth Wilson realized that she had this problem. She noticed she didn't have many close relationships. It wasn't that she didn't like people. She had a lot of friends, but as soon as friendships developed to a certain depth, she would avoid the person. "I was so scared of real relationships," she said, "scared that I would have to give my entire testimony, and ultimately not be accepted, scared that I would become vulnerable and be left." On her kingdom journey, she realized God accepted her whole story, even the bad parts. It made it possible for her to be vulnerable. "That Ruth is gone," she said. "It's all or nothing now."

WE NEED TO GRIEVE

When kingdom journeys do their job, they take us to a place where we see our brokenness and from there, God's dependable faithfulness. To move past brokenness, we need to be able to grieve. Without true grief — mourning our broken parts — we can't move on.

Journeys lead people into brokenness. People leave brokenness through grieving.

No one wants to invite grief. Usually it comes looking for you. But, push it away, refuse to feel its depths, or keep it where it can't touch you and you will be stunted emotionally. You will limit your ability to be free in *joy* when it comes. A refusal to embrace grief is the emotional equivalent of folding your arms across your body and holding yourself more tightly. Your folded arms can't fly.

When we lose someone or something we hold dear — we break inside. We feel the brokenness and we have to grieve. Grieving is hard work. People need to be shown how to grieve or maybe how to give themselves permission to grieve. Patience is a key resource as the grief process does its healing work.

A lot of people are stuck coming to grips with their brokenness. A lot of folks have never exited those broken places through a healthy grief process.

What does this look like? It looks like Susan. "I lived so long thinking I was ugly and unlovable," she said. "For years I shut others out, rejecting them before they rejected me. Truthfully, people did want to love me. I wasted all those years and can never get them back." She can't get the years back, but Susan was able to move on when she grieved her wasted years. And she won't waste any more.

Stephanie Pridgen says, "We talked so much about grieving on my kingdom journey that it made you want to scream. But it was so necessary." She elaborated, "Even in the midst of knowing this, when I went to Ukraine this year, I popped into the culture without really grieving what I was leaving behind (family, friends, culture, language, Chick-fil-A). Around month three I had a total meltdown. For a few weeks I was constantly on the verge of tears and kind of thought I had made the wrong decision in going. Friends from home would tell me of situations and I would feel that

I couldn't do anything and I should be there to help. It was then I realized that I never grieved the leaving, letting go of all that I expected and found comfortable, trusting God with friends and families."

HOW TO GRIEVE

Ron Walborn says that we all need to write a grief journal.[44] He suggests journaling about our losses and our feelings about them. It's a biblical concept. The book of Lamentations is a grief journal. Jeremiah lost everything and poured his tears out on paper, journaling thoughts such as, "The Lord is like an enemy; he has swallowed up Israel" (Lamentations 2:5).

Jeremiah's outpouring of grief isn't blasphemy. This is the kind of healthy grieving more of us need to do. God encourages it. The alternative is to allow our grief to go un-expressed, festering into bitterness and even hate. To be human means to suffer loss. We lose our grandparents and eventually our parents. All of us lose our youth and with it our taut skin and vigor. Many of us lose our dreams. Our friends fall away. Some of us make poor choices and lose our integrity. Others suffer catastrophic loss when a child dies.

To be human is to have joy and hope robbed from you. We have a sworn enemy who lives to see this happen and who always looks for a "twofer," tempting us to live in a prison of bitterness after he's stolen our joy.

Counselor Gary Collins describes seven aids to grieving:

1. Embrace the feelings. Admit the pain. Give yourself permission to grieve.

2. Don't rush. Recovery and renewal are more like steady growth with periodic setbacks.

3. Stay encouraged. Keep in contact with others who are supportive but who can gently and sensitively push you forward.

4. Say no to revenge. Don't dwell on getting even. It slows the recovery process.

5. Exercise, even when you don't feel like it. Exercise can help your body and brain resist illness, think more clearly, fight depression, and foster a more positive attitude.

6. Keep learning. This is something that we can control. It has been suggested that "use it or lose it" applies to every part of your body, mind, and social life.

7. Talk to God. Communicate with him regularly, even if you doubt his presence or his awareness of your circumstances.

8. Dream. Keeping visions alive can help us all grow beyond the past and move forward to a positive future.[45]

WATCHING OUT FOR GOD

Shawn had grown up next door to us in Florida. He was one of my son, Seth's, best friends. When we moved to Georgia, our families stayed in touch. He earned his master's degree in psychology and mental health.

When Shawn learned his mother was dying of ovarian cancer, he called me and asked if he could come to stay with us. His mom was a great woman and a good friend. Her illness was tearing Shawn and his family apart and he needed to find some clarity.

Shawn left his home and drove several hundred miles with nothing on his agenda except to experience God and process what had happened. A few days later, he was at my house along with a group of young men I disciple. We happened to be talking about kingdom journeys. When I told Shawn he was on something of a kingdom journey, he enthusiastically agreed. "That's exactly what I am doing," he said. "I knew even before I left that I was going on a spiritual journey."

Earlier that day, Shawn had been driving back from the grocery store when he heard an almost audible word from the Lord to "pull the car to the side of the road." The voice was so stern it shocked him. Shawn immediately drove to a parking lot and turned off his car.

"Move aside," God spoke. That was it. Shawn thought about it some, then started the car and finished his drive home.

Shawn arrived at our house, stunned and confused. He felt God wanted to do something, but Shawn felt he was somehow stopping it from happening. He didn't know what he was in the way of and he didn't know how to get out of the way.

As we talked and prayed, Shawn grew more convinced God was going to do something. With his mom dying of cancer, he hoped God was going to help her. Shawn needed to be ready.

God was calling Shawn to stand on the watchtower and wait, to look expectantly for God to move. Standing on the watchtower; is actively passive. It is active in the sense that the watchman must show up, but passive in that he isn't supposed to do anything other than watch.

Often we want to control God. We ask him to show up when we want him and to fix the problems we want fixed. Shawn may have wanted this, but God was calling him to get out of the way. God was saying, "Open the gate of your heart, stand on the watchtower, and get ready for me to move" (Isaiah 21:8).

Kingdom journey sensitizes us to what God is doing. As our spiritual eyes begin to take in new sights, as we experience new cultures, we begin to see God moving in and around us. On a kingdom journey, we become the watchmen on the tower, searching to see what God is doing. Sometimes we discover him in the midst of pain. Sometimes we discover him after pain is gone. But inevitably, when we experience pain, he uses it.

When we search for God, we feel pain, discomfort, and exhaustion. We will want to leave the watchtower, take cover and find a place of comfort. We will want to find some relief. A journey destabilizes us so that it's harder to escape. In a foreign country, we don't have as much control over our environment as we do at home. When we're hungry, we may not be able to find a fast-food restaurant for a cheap, quick snack. When we're bored, we can't turn on the television. You have to feel the pain. You have to go through it. Kingdom journey makes it more difficult to leave the watchtower.

Waiting on God is hard work. Sometimes, the distractions and comforts must be excised from your life so you can wait attentively. It takes strength to say no to the things that distract you from God. Knowing that on the other side of brokenness is hope, restoration, and renewal, we do well to press into the pain. His words to us are, "Embrace brokenness for the gift that it is. Push through the process until it's complete."

SETTING PEOPLE FREE

God will not waste the pain of your brokenness. He often will use it to help someone else. Take Erin, for example. Her journey allowed her uninvited brokenness to bring freedom to others.

"I was raped in 2008," Erin told a classroom of thirty-five

girls in Kenya, "and I thank God for it, because I can comfort other girls who have experienced it. I am here to tell you that in Christ, there is hope, healing, and victory."

How could she be thankful that she went through such a horrible, emotionally scarring experience like rape? She couldn't — until she saw that God would use her experience to bring healing to other girls.

After giving her testimony, Erin sat down. Some of the girls had their heads on their desks. The feeling in the room was heavy. One of the Kenyan women in charge asked if anyone else would like to give a testimony.

A young girl stood up timidly. "I am your peer," she said. "You know me very well. You know my smile. I wear this smile so that no one knows this has happened to me. I have never told anyone this before. But I too am a victim of rape. It was my uncle."

Many of the girls in the room began to weep. The young girl who shared her testimony put her head in her hands, unable to make eye contact with anyone. The team asked the girls to raise their hands if they too had been raped and wanted freedom through prayer. Nearly all of the girls raised their hands. Erin and her teammates began to pray for each girl, one-by-one, inviting healing, and seeking freedom.

You can push brokenness down like a beach ball under the water, but it eventually seeks the surface. Brokenness begins to show itself when we take off the smile we wear around our peers. We see its reality when we admit we are not fine. Life is not okay. We may prefer to keep the pain inside hidden, but when we're honest about it, we make room for healing to occur.

You don't have to go on a kingdom journey to experience brokenness, but it helps. God sent every major hero in the Bible on a journey so they could be broken. David ran from Saul and was broken along the way. Elijah was driven to the wilderness for two years. Abraham left his father's tent and spent the rest of his life in the desert. Jonah had to throw himself off the ship that he was using to flee God before he was broken. Paul lived a life of journeying that began with blindness and a rebuke. Jesus started his three-year journey to the cross with a forty-day sojourn in the wilderness that left him so depleted the angels had to minister to him.

Henri Nouwen says it well,

> "We live with broken bodies, broken hearts, broken minds, or broken spirits. We suffer from broken relationships. How can we live with our brokenness? Jesus invites us to embrace our brokenness as he embraced the cross and live it as part of our mission. He asks us not to reject our brokenness as a curse from God that reminds us of our sinfulness, but to accept it and put it under God's blessing for our purification and sanctification. Thus, our brokenness can become a gateway to new life."[46]

JESUS IS BROKEN

Mallorie Miller had been devastated by her day in the hospital in Swaziland. She was haunted by the image of the woman in the brown sweater mourning her dead child. Mallorie's mind was filled with questions about God's character, about his ability to handle her pain, and the world's pain. Her journey had led her into brokenness, but she didn't know how she would ever move beyond that place of pain.

Later that night, Mallorie closed her eyes and saw a vision of Jesus. He was walking through the Manzini hospital. The woman in the brown sweater was lying on the floor, still weeping. Jesus went to her and put his arms around her. Then, he took up her baby and held it.

The vision gave Mallorie hope. It allowed her to accept her own brokenness.

"I knew it was okay to hurt," she said later, "and that Jesus understood, more than I could."

If we do not embrace brokenness for what it is, we remain stuck, unable to arrive. If we don't do the work to understand how God wants to redeem it, we are left in that pit, weeping… wondering where God is.

Brokenness, like the larger kingdom journey, can be a wonderful gift when we're able to embrace our broken places. After all, brokenness is merely a temporary way station on the road to healing.

CHAPTER 9 NOTES

43. Quoted in Dan Rockwell, "10 Ways to Become a Risk-Taker," *LeadershipFreak.wordpress.com,* http://www.leadershipfreak.wordpress.com/2012/04/10/10-ways-to-become-a-risk-taker.

44. Ron Walborn, *Grieving the Seasons of Our Lives,* podcast audio. Personal Spiritual Formation, MP3, 50. http://www.adventures.org/podcasts/psf/grievingtheseasonsofourlives.mp3.

45. Gary R. Collins, "Starting Over," *Gary R. Collins,* no. 335 (2009), http://www.garyrcollins.com/newsletter.php?letterid=34.

46. Henri Nouwen, *Bread for the Journey,* (San Francisco: HarperCollins, 1997), 197.

CHAPTER 10: DEPENDENCE

"We are a long time in learning that all our strength and salvation is in God." — David Brainerd[47]

For years, Andrew Maas wanted to go on a kingdom journey. He talked about it time and time again, but his family and friends always said, "It's too dangerous. You're too young." On top of that, Andrew was afraid he couldn't depend on God. Where would he sleep? What would he eat? What if God didn't come through?

Andrew was working as a bike taxi driver in West Palm Beach, Florida, when someone told him about the Passion Conference near Dallas, Texas. Immediately, he knew the conference was his chance to take a risky, faith-building journey.

Andrew determined to follow Jesus' Luke 10 protocol — taking no food, no money, and no extra clothes. He talked about it with friends, and one made the commitment to go all the way to Texas with him.

They had eighteen days before the conference started. As Andrew and his friend prayed about their journey, they decided they would get bikes and ride them the 1,300 miles to the conference. They were going out just like the disciples of Luke 10 and they would have to depend on God to provide for their needs every moment of their journey.

A week before his trip to the Passion Conference, Andrew still didn't have a bike. The cheapest road bike he could find was $840, too expensive for him to buy. The bike Andrew envisioned was rusty, old, and looked like it was only being held together by the grace of God.

"I felt like God was impressing upon me that he wanted me to get a bike that when people saw it they would say, 'You are going to Texas on that?' I was beginning to learn that God likes to use things that give him the glory. There is a reason why he uses the least likely people for great things in his kingdom."

God didn't make it easy — he put Andrew's faith to the test. The day before Andrew and his friend were supposed to leave for the conference, he still hadn't found his bike. He went from thrift shop to thrift shop looking for it. He was checking out his last shop and about to give up when he saw it glistening in the window: a gold, rusty Schwinn that looked like it was from the 1970s. This was a bike that would require dependence. Andrew spent the whole night restoring it. The next day he was up before dawn, taking the bike to the beach.

Andrew dipped his tired-looking wheels into the Atlantic Ocean as a kind of baptism and then set off, counting down the miles to Texas. While his friend had all kinds of problems with his bike — flat tires and lost screws — Andrew rode hundreds of miles problem-free.

God seems to prefer these kinds of odds. Our dependence

on him allows him to reveal his power through us. Because Andrew was willing to look foolish, God got the glory.

LEARNING TO DEPEND ON GOD

When Keturah Weathers returned from her kingdom journey in December 2010, people told her, "I think it's great what you did, but I could never do that."

Keturah would reply, "Yeah, I could never do what I did, either. That's the point. God gives us grace. When we embark on something he has called us to do, he takes us beyond ourselves."

This is the language of trust: Jesus said, "Do not worry about your life, what you will eat or drink; or about your body, what you will wear. Is not life more than food and the body more than clothes?" God will take care of you — not just your spiritual needs, but also your physical needs.

We don't need much to be content. The apostle Paul was content in the midst of beatings, shipwrecks, long trips by foot, and imprisonment. He was content because he trusted that God would give him everything he needed, but not necessarily everything he wanted.

Like Keturah and Andrew, we sometimes can't help asking questions of the Lord: "If I trust you alone, will you take care of me?" "Will you give me enough to eat?" "Will you give me a place to live?" "What about my car payment and my college loans?" We wonder if God really will come through for us as he does in the Bible. We wonder how we could ever have radical dependence like the early disciples.

We usually learn to depend on God when we have to do so. When you've got nothing left to lose, it's easier to turn him. Dependence is a discipline we develop in concert with God.

How do we learn to depend on God? It's a little more difficult when life doesn't require dependence. You can wait until a crisis shows up in your life or you can start before then. You can go on a kingdom journey, for example, that requires you to abandon everything. With no other resources, you are forced to depend on the Lord to come through in miraculous ways. At the point where God is all you have, he will become all you need. Through this process, you will learn to listen to his voice and obey.

Jesus intentionally modeled dependence so his disciples could see what it looked like. "The Son can do nothing by himself," he told them in John 5:19. "He can do only what he sees his Father doing, because whatever the Father does the Son also does." After the disciples watched Jesus depend on the Father, he sent them on a kingdom journey of their own to learn without him to fall back on. They walked through the towns and villages of Judea with nothing extra so that they could experience God's kingdom on their own. It was not enough to merely watch someone else journey and know how to do it; they needed an experience to make it real in their own lives. Studying how to swim is different than actually learning to swim.

For those of us who live in America, one of the wealthiest countries in the world, this concept of dependence can be a struggle. It is for me. The reality is I don't *have* to trust him. I have everything I need — enough money, enough food, and adequate shelter. Usually, without really having to trust him for my "daily bread," it still ends up on the table. Thus, I too easily default to a position of self-sufficiency. Without fresh evidence of his provision, my faith begins to weaken — I'm not as sure about his trustworthiness as I once was. "Will he show up that way again?" I ask myself. Spiritual entropy begins to set in.

So what do I do? I force myself into situations that require trust in God.

Before setting out on their 1300-mile journey, Andrew decided on a very specific strategy to learn this kind of dependence. He and his friend chose not to make a plan. There would be no daily distance goal. They wouldn't decide in advance which cities they would stop in. And, of course, since they didn't have any money, there were no hotels to check into along the way.

Andrew says most of their prayers sounded like, "Lord, take us to the people that you want us to meet to bring glory to your name." And, "Lord, give us safety as we travel." Their only plan was to figure out God's plan.

They also had a rule — they would never ask for food. On the first day they stopped near five or six trucks parked by an orange orchard. They got into a conversation with the drivers and told them what they were doing. Andrew and his friend didn't ask for anything, but the drivers gave them a few oranges apiece. After biking so far with nothing to eat, the oranges were delicious! "When you have no idea where your next meal is coming from, there is a certain sense of gratefulness about it," Andrew said. Not only did God feed them by putting them in a place of dependence, the gifts he gave them were actually more enjoyable.

GOD WANTS TO BE YOUR PARTNER

God wants a partnership with us. He doesn't want us to be autonomous. He wants to be Lord of our lives. We call Jesus "Lord" so much that the word has lost its meaning. It means that he wants to be involved in our decision-making. Not only does he want us to ask him about the big things — like who to marry, what job offer to accept, or where we should go to college. He also wants us to consult him on the little things. Yes, he wants us to ask where we should park our car, what to eat for dinner, and whether to work an extra five minutes on a project. He wants us to consult with him, just as we would our best friends and family. He wants us to depend on him.

Some Christians misinterpret this and won't make a move unless God tells them. Another group of believers fails to involve him at all in their decision-making. Neither approach is biblical. God wants us to live in the paradox of "my power is made perfect in weakness." He wants to partner with us.

This is the language of dependence — of having to rely on God because you are bankrupt. In a land founded on independence, dependence is a concept most of us struggle to understand. Everything in me wants to be self-sufficient. And that's the problem, my posture is incompatible with the idea of a God who wants to display his power through me, especially in my weakness.

I don't know where you are weak, but I know where I am. For example, I've stubbed my toe enough relationally to know I can be insensitive. This is most obviously apparent in the familiar places of life… where I let my guard down — in my home, and especially in my marriage. At first, it was rough sledding for my wife, Karen, and me. Slowly, I came to understand how this issue of insensitivity affected her. Out of love for her, I needed to change my style. God didn't miraculously give me the gift of tact. As I listened, God began to whisper to me more about how to be soft when I just wanted to "tell it like it is."

The good news is that this weakness of mine makes me a candidate to partner with and lean on God. The bad news is: I don't feel much like being close to God or anybody else on days when I wake up feeling irritable. I feel prickly and unlovable and forlornly human. There is little in me that wants to love anything. If there is one cup of coffee left in the pot, I can't be trusted to not to fight Karen for it. Knowing this about myself drives me to pray and ask God for help. It's me being broken, but also moving from brokenness to dependence.

We are self-sufficient by nature. We have to be taught how to depend on our Lord. This is why the American Dream is so at odds with the Christian life. The American Dream is about security and comfort. But the two cars, the house, the nice job, and 401k, can release us from the need to depend on God. These are not "bad" in and of themselves, but they anesthetize us to the spiritual realities around us.

Jesus told his disciples to pray for their daily bread. When you need God to this degree, it gives you the opportunity to see his goodness as he provides. That, in turn, enables you to trust him more in the future. This is not the kind of dependence you can learn in a classroom or church pew. This kind of dependence can only be learned in the real world, walking with Christ.

LIKE A SON

Jesus always modeled a discipline for his disciples and then tested them in it. Their kingdom journeys were tests to see whether they had learned to depend on God as Jesus did. On the first go-around, they had their master as backup, but eventually, they had to do it on their own. It had to have changed the way they understood God. Perhaps for the first time, they were able to see God as their true Father, the one who provided for *all* their needs. This is what happened with Joe Bunting.

Two months into Joe's journey, he was forced to depend on God to take care of his physical needs. He was in Budapest, Hungary. His team arrived in the city with no plans, no contacts, and not enough money to afford expensive European hostels. Joe relied on God to find a place to stay for him and his six travel partners to manage a meager budget of eight dollars per person per night. Most of the hostels were booked. The few that had space were charging much more than they could afford. By dusk, they were still looking for a place to stay. Budapest began to look bleak.

"I was preparing myself to spend the night on the street," Joe recalled. "I was feeling a mixture of panic and peace. I kept thinking of the Hungarian police coming up to us at three in the morning telling us we couldn't sleep on the streets. Then where would we go? We were all praying hard that God would find us a place to stay." Joe had found himself in the middle of the unknown — the very spot where we often find God.

One of Joe's teammates stumbled on a place renting out luxury apartments. They ended up with two apartments for the price of one, complete with full kitchen, flat-screen television, and free movie rentals. Everyone had their own bedroom, an amazing blessing for a group of backpackers trekking through Europe. Somehow, all of this met their minimal budget.

"That was one of the highest spiritual moments of my kingdom journey," Joe said. "I had never experienced God as a provider, as my Father, like I did that night. It wasn't the TV or the apartments that made me happy. It was that I was God's child — he took care of me far beyond my expectations. I understood the idea of being like a son intellectually before, but that night I got it on a whole other level."

Joe depended upon God. God provided magnificently. The team's faith and trust in God hit a new high after their ability to rely on themselves hit a new low.

CHILDLIKE FAITH

Bethany Brueggen discovered this side of God when she was in Phuket, Thailand. She had been ministering to the prostitutes in the bars and clubs of the red-light district. One day, she was asked to give a devotional about depending on God to a group of women who had recently left the bars.

Bethany spent hours thinking of what to say, but nothing came. What do you say to someone who has experienced such pain? What hope can you give to a woman who is forced to sell her body for a pittance? Finally, she gave up and just asked God for a Bible verse. She didn't hear anything until just before she was supposed to talk. Finally, he spoke to her and gave her Matthew 6:25-33, which begins with: "Do not worry about your life, what you will eat or what you will drink" and concludes with: "Seek first his kingdom."

From there, she was inspired to talk about having the faith of a child, a faith that depends entirely on God. "I talked about how a little girl comes to her father," Bethany said, "desperate and unable to do anything for herself. She comes without fear and she comes knowing that her father will provide for her when she can't provide for herself."

Her devotional was also a personal challenge to listen to her own advice. "I felt convicted, and I asked the Lord to increase my own faith. I felt like he wanted to begin preparing me for a lifetime of radical trust and dependence."

That same day, Bethany lost her debit card and was unable to withdraw money from the bank. She could have borrowed money from one of the girls she was traveling with, but she felt like God wanted her to depend on him to provide for her. In the afternoon, she had planned to go into town to buy toothpaste. Since she couldn't get money out of the bank, she only had enough for the bus fare into town — forty baht (about $1.00 US). She didn't have enough money for toothpaste or even bus fare back home.

This was her chance to put her Father to the test. If he didn't come through, she would be stuck far from home without any money, without a cell phone, where almost no one spoke English. Knowing this, she got on the bus, gave up the forty baht for the fare and put herself in a place where her only choice was to trust God.

When Bethany arrived in town, she stepped into a coffee shop to use the Internet and read her Bible. The shop required customers to purchase a drink before they could get online. Bethany, of course, couldn't afford to buy a drink. She knew that if she were going to use the Internet, God would have to buy her a drink. So, she sat down and opened up her Bible. Almost immediately, a couple from Australia who were sitting next to her asked if she was a Christian. She told them she was and they asked what she was doing in Thailand. She told them about her kingdom journey and about her ministry with the prostitutes in Phuket.

"It was an encouraging conversation," Bethany recounted. "Doing ministry in the bars wore on me. I was feeling discouraged about it." When the couple showed enthusiasm about her work in Phuket, she was re-energized. She remembered how important her work was and she thanked God for sending someone to encourage her. "Besides that, they had the cutest baby in the world." When the couple got up to leave, Bethany was excited to go back to the bars that night.

She continued to read her Bible at the coffee shop and a few minutes later the Australian couple returned. They asked if she would be offended by a financial gift. They said that they had both felt God leading them to come back and bless her.

"Of course not," she said, realizing immediately that God was answering her prayers. The couple gave her 1000 baht (about $30) enough for a dozen tubes of toothpaste and the bus fare home. Bethany was so excited that she told the family the whole story, crying as she explained how she had lost her bank card and felt God leading her to depend on him as a child depends on her father. After encouraging her, they left, and Bethany said goodbye through tears of gratitude

Ten minutes later, the couple came back again. They said they felt God leading them to give her even more! They handed her an Australian hundred-dollar bill (about $95.00 US). "My child-like faith exploded," she said. "My Abba Father is so good to me. I only asked for a tube of toothpaste!" But her father had given her so much more.

JESUS ALSO HAD TO LEARN DEPENDENCE

Let's look at Jesus. Even as a twelve-year-old kid, Jesus understood he had to be about his Father's business. Later in life, as a prophet, preacher, and miracle worker, his dependence on God was complete. "By myself I can do nothing; I judge only as I hear," he says in John 5:30.

When we look at Jesus we see that he depended on God in two ways:

1. To meet his physical needs

2. To lead his kingdom work

In other words, Jesus trusted God with his input and output, his receiving and giving.

To build God's kingdom, we have to learn dependence. It's how we begin to activate our faith. Jesus modeled the kind of ministry that his followers needed to imitate. If the Son of Man had to learn dependence on the Father, then so must we.

In Ephesians 2:10, Paul says that God has stored up good works for us to do. If we are to do those good works, we must learn to pay attention to what we see and hear the Father doing; we must learn how to depend on him.

We need to plug into another power source if we are to come close to doing what Jesus did. Dependence is the plug connecting us to divine power — it's that place in our kingdom journey where we experience another level of grace.

How do we practice dependence in ministry? We know that the Lord always wants to rescue the lost, heal the sick, and set the captives free. So we might begin by asking him for his heart of compassion. Like Jesus, we can ask God where he's working and how we can join him. Of course, the real test comes when we step out in obedience to what we see and hear him doing. The more frequently we risk trusting him to show up, the more he'll prove himself trustworthy.

GOD DOESN'T MAKE IT EASY

Andrew and his friend trusted God to provide for them as they cycled over a thousand miles to the Passion conference. Along the way, God more than provided. Over the course of the journey, they received close to a thousand dollars in gifts from churches and strangers, even a couple of dollars from a winning lottery ticket they found discarded on the roadside.

A few days before they arrived at the conference, they felt God's tug to abandon everything all over again. Andrew and his friend gave away the hundreds of dollars they had, dropping huge chunks of small bills in offering plates. They gave jars of peanut butter to homeless people they met along the way. In fact, they gave away so much that by the time they arrived in Dallas, they didn't have enough money to pay for the $80 conference tickets.

Once more the temptation loomed before Andrew to disbelieve God. Yes, by depending upon him they had seen God provide over and over again. But maybe this time was different. Would God provide now? The conference was starting and they had no tickets.

In Dallas, Andrew sat outside of Wal-Mart guarding the bikes when a small group of people stopped to talk to him.

"Where are you going?" they asked.

"To the Passion Conference."

"To Passion? Oh. We're the directors of Passion."

Andrew was stunned. He told them all about the eighteen-day journey and how God had provided. The directors were so amazed that they gave Andrew and his friend free tickets to the conference. Thirty thousand people joined Andrew at the Passion Conference that year. The verse that embedded itself into Andrew's heart over the weekend was Matthew 6:33, "Seek first his kingdom and his righteousness, and all these things will be added to you as well." Andrew learned to abandon, but not only that — he learned to depend on God.

Our self-sufficiency is at odds with a God who wants to display his power through us. The Lord tends to use us in ways that make it clear he's working, not us. For instance, God usually empowers me in areas where I am obviously flawed. He wants people to realize that it's not me doing the work. This way, God gets the glory and not me.

I try to be transparent about my brokenness. By allowing people to see my flaws, I find God uses them to set people free — free from comparison, free from needing to be perfect, and free from self-condemnation.

We take our cue from our master. Something has to die if people are ever to be set free. By sharing our weaknesses and failings, our own dignity may take a hit, but others are encouraged to consider themselves differently. If Jesus hadn't suffered so much in death, his resurrection wouldn't have been as significant.

Kingdom journey works so well as a spiritual discipline because it leads us to abandonment, brokenness, and dependence. We leave everything, lose everything, and then, empty-handed, receive *everything* back again. Along the way, God reveals his glory through us. The experience is transforming. You can't help loving and trusting a God like that.

RESCUING THE LOST

Marisa Banas had been on her kingdom journey a number of months when her world was turned upside down, taking her to places of complete dependence.

"Marisa, do you have a first aid kit? The kid in the purple shirt cut his hand pretty bad." This was Marisa's introduction to Allan, the boy who would dominate her thoughts and prayers for a month in Kenya... and long after she left.

Allan ran away from his abusive mother when he was nine years old. He wore a purple shirt, torn and stained from three years of living on the street. On his hand was a long, infected gash. Like most street kids in Kenya, Allan obsessively clung to his bottle of glue, lifting it to his mouth every few seconds to inhale its noxious gas in order to stay high.

Not only did Marisa take care of his cut, she contacted a nearby orphanage and arranged to bring Allan there. By the end of the month, Allan was settling in to his new home, the Challenge Farm. The mother of the home welcomed Allan with open arms. He even knew two of the kids there. Marisa had rescued him.

Of course, when you tell the story this way, it sounds easy. It leaves out all the twists and turns. You don't see Marisa almost losing hope that she would be able to help Allan at all. You miss the very real threat that Allan could have been beaten up and killed by the other street kids. Not to mention, Marisa had no contacts in any orphanages in Kenya. She didn't have any money to support him at the orphanage, either. When you look at the whole story, the odds seem impossible. Allan only made it to Challenge Farm because Marisa depended on God. God made it happen through Marisa.

Kingdom journey is a process of emptying, so that we can be filled with the fullness of God's Spirit. Dependence begins the filling part. The first two stages show us that our own resources are inadequate. Only God can do what needs to be done.

For Marisa, God was working through her in one of the projects closest to his heart: orphans and widows. "Religion that God our Father accepts as pure and faultless is this," says James 1:27, "to look after orphans and widows in their distress and to keep oneself from being polluted by the world."

God cares about orphans and widows precisely because they have no one else to depend on. As we reach out to them, we become God's representatives. Their dependence on God can rub off on us; we become more dependent by helping those who are most dependent on God.

This is what makes the rest of Marisa's story so amazing. She came to the place on her kingdom journey where she was completely bankrupt. If God didn't get Allan into Challenge Farm, it wouldn't get done.

PRESUMPTION OR FAITH?

Many street kids like Allan aren't true orphans. They are often raised by single mothers. When their mothers can't afford to feed them or when a new boyfriend doesn't want them around, the kids move out and take to the street.

While Marisa volunteered with a church in the slums of Eldoret, Kenya, Allan was one of more than 250,000 kids living on the Kenyan streets. When someone called her over to look at Allan's cut hand, she brought her friend Jess, who was an Army nurse.

Marisa and Jess inspected Allan's wound, a deep slice in his hand that had become infected. Marisa cleaned it and then Jess stitched it up. They left him that day and told him to keep his wound clean. Marisa worried about him all night, wondering how a twelve-year-old living on the street could take care of a wound. How could he even take care of himself?

The next day, Marisa was at the host church when Allan found her. She took him under her wing and decided to take responsibility to keep his wound clean. "I went into 'mama mode,'" she said. "Before I knew it, he became my son."

Marisa decided she needed to give Allan a bath and wash his clothes. First, she went to the supermarket to buy soap, Allan trailing behind her. Then, they walked through the dump to a river behind the church where she could wash Allan's clothes and he could bathe. This was the first time that his clothes had ever been washed. As she scrubbed them clean, she watched Allan take a few big huffs from his bottle of glue. Her heart broke at the thought of the damage the glue was doing to his body and soul.

Later, she told her translator, Meshack, "Allan needs a father."

"Okay," he said. "I will take him home to my mother. She will take care of him."

Marisa was surprised and relieved. Had God found Allan his new father? But from the first hours, Allan's presence in Meshack's home caused problems.

Marisa walked Allan around the neighborhood so he could meet the kids who lived there. As it began to get late, she took him back to Meschack's small, unlit apartment. Then, she realized that Meshack's mother wasn't cooking anything for dinner. "Meshack, has Mama already eaten?" Marisa asked. Meshack's face fell.

"There is no food," Meshack said.

Marisa replied, "How often does your mother eat?"

"Only when I can bring food. Marisa, I have no job."

Meshack's words felt like a ton of bricks falling on Marisa. She knew that with no food, Allan would go back to the streets and scrounging through the trash in a glue-sniffing daze. He'd likely become disenchanted towards anyone who would try to help him in the future.

On top of that, Marisa knew how dangerous it was for a street kid to return to street-life after being rescued, especially when they were taken off the streets by white missionaries, as Allan had been. The other street kids would expect him to have received money from the missionaries. Out of their jealousy, they would likely attack Allan.

"All of these serious threats haunted me," said Marisa. "His life or death was in my hands. I thought, 'Oh, God. What have I done?'"

Marisa took Allan back to the house where she was staying. She had a few weeks left before she had to leave. She needed to find a more permanent home for him, quickly. Marissa spent a night on her knees in prayer. She had reached her place of brokenness, the end of her own resources. If God didn't come through, Allan would go back to the streets, alone and vulnerable.

"I felt like a fool as I replayed the past couple of days' activities over and over," she recalled. "Did we move in presumption or was it faith?"

DEPENDENCE REQUIRES RISK

Up to this point, Marisa had taken a lot of risks. First, she left everything she knew, all the comfort of her home in Wisconsin.

Risk is crucial to kingdom journey. The disciples had nothing on their journey — no acoustic guitars, no video projectors to show the Jesus Film, not even a backpack. All they had was a message and a blessing. Yet, they were able to cast demons out of people, heal the sick, and raise the dead. It makes you wonder if perhaps we depend too much on props and not enough on the God who created the heavens and the earth.

The amazing thing is that God wants to live through us *at all*. We were created from dust, but he made us heirs, inheritors of his glory. He doesn't want us to have any doubts about his role in our lives. He doesn't want us hedging our bets. He tells us in Malachi, "Test me." Why? Because he wants to prove himself trustworthy and he wants us to trust him.

God loves the eleventh hour. He wants the piggy bank emptied. He doesn't want a fair fight. He took Gideon's army from 30,000 to 10,000 to 300. He set David, the country shepherd, against Goliath, the war hero. He gave twelve men — with little or no education, wealth, or particular talent — the incomprehensibly huge assignment of turning the world upside down. Why does he do this? Perhaps it's so the impossible odds prove *his* power.

When we avoid risk or compromise, God doesn't live through us to the extent that he'd like. He wants us to depend on him and his resources. To accomplish God-sized dreams, we must jump into situations where we have to depend on him.

THE FINAL HOUR

As Marisa wrestled with what to do, God spoke to her in a dream. She saw a vision of God writing one word on her forehead: "Determination." Later he spoke to her, saying, "Marisa will you stop trusting me now? Get up and believe."

Four days after taking him off the streets, Marisa was walking Allan home after buying a new set of clean clothes for him. The "before" and "after" pictures were profound — a dirty, glue-sniffing street kid was turned into a clean, beloved son. As they walked, a homeless man started to follow them, talking roughly to Allan.

Something erupted inside of Marisa, surprising the homeless man, Allan, and even herself. She began to defend Allan from the man, who then turned away from him and toward her. He grabbed her hands and shouted at her, "Buy me clothes!"

She glared at him and shouted back, "No!" When she ripped his hands off her, the man melted away. Stirred by the violence of the encounter, Marisa found Meshack and wagged her finger in his face, "Allan cannot go back to the streets. Do you hear me?!"

Marisa, Meshack, and the pastor of the church where she was volunteering searched desperately to find Allan a safe place to live. One Sunday, a few days before she was supposed to leave, Marisa was going to preach at the church. At the last second, the translator canceled. But a man spoke up from the back: "I'll translate for you."

He stood up and walked forward. At first, Marisa thought he was an angel. He wore clean, new clothes unlike most of the parishioners who lived in the slums and dressed in rags. His name was David. She was impressed with his perfect English and his zeal for the Lord. "What is he doing in our slum?" she thought.

After church, David started asking Marisa questions. She shared her inability to find a good home for Allan. David grew animated. Excitedly, he told her about an orphanage, Challenge Farm. It was outside of the city and run by Americans.

As they talked, he became so concerned about Allan and his plight that he decided to use his Christmas vacation time to find out more information about the orphanage. Marisa wondered again if David were an angel. She even pinched him to see if he was real.

On January 2, the day before she was supposed to leave, Marisa was able to contact a woman named Grace at Challenge Farm. When she asked Grace if Allan could live at the orphanage, Grace enthusiastically replied, "Yes! Bring the child!"

Marisa was thrilled. It looked as though Allan would finally have a home. The pressing problem was time. Marisa still needed to take Allan to an orphanage she'd never seen, hoping it would be right for him.

They left at sunrise so that they could return in time for Marisa to catch the bus. As they rode the three-hour trip to Challenge Farm, Marisa looked at Allan in the backseat, clean and smiling. She couldn't believe it was the same glue-sniffing street kid she had met only weeks before. As she watched him, her heart beat with fear. She started thinking, "What happens if this doesn't work out? What will we do with him then?" But there was no room for "what-ifs." She had to put her trust in God; there were no other options.

As soon as she met Grace, Marisa knew God had answered all of her prayers for Allan and had arranged the perfect situation for him. "I see all the children on the streets, and I wish I could take them all in," said Grace. "If only I had enough beds!"

When he entered the farm, Allan immediately recognized two boys who had also been rescued from life on the street. A crowd of kids gathered around him. Grace told them, "This is Allan. He wants to come live here. Should I let him?"

"Yes!" the kids shouted at once.

"No," said Grace, teasingly. "No, I think I will send him back."

"No! We have more beds!" the kids said, worried looks on their faces. They started grabbing Allan's things so she couldn't send him back. Allan had found a home.

One year later, Marisa returned to Kenya to visit Challenge Farm. When she arrived, Marisa gave Allan a scrapbook of pictures documenting his move from the streets to the farm the year before. The next day, she took Allan and four other kids who were sick to the clinic. He was so attached to his scrapbook that he brought it with him to the clinic. In the waiting room, the adults asked about the book. Allan showed them the pictures and answered their questions. They all were shocked to see the transformation that had taken place in him over a year. One woman looked through the book several times while showering Allan with questions. When Marisa asked what Allan was saying, the woman told her, "The child is ministering to me. Look at what God has done with his life."

Looking back at it all, Marisa said, "The lesson that I have learned is to obey. Even when you can't figure it out in your mind, just obey! God really is faithful."

SELF-SUFFICIENCY HAS TO GO

I was raised to believe self-reliance was a positive trait. Maybe you were, too. However, we would do well to ask ourselves the question, "Am I moving toward isolation and self-reliance or toward greater dependence on God and others?" We may think we need to deal with these things on our own. But really what we need is to allow God and his church to help us find answers.

"We've been force-fed the doctrine of self-reliance for so long that it's embedded into the very fabric of our souls," say authors Jerry Bridges and Bob Bevington.[48] The irony, according to Bridges, is that the more God-given abilities we have, the more we're prone to rely on them — rather than on God. The problem is this self-reliance is corrosive to our souls.

We may not even be aware of our baggage. Too many of us slog through life under a cloud, weighed down and depressed by responsibilities and burdens. We fail to realize that we were meant to share the load.

Let me invite you to consider that it may be time to give up on self-reliance. You weren't meant to go through life alone. Relying on God and others doesn't mean life will be easy, but it is essential if we're to find the life we were meant to live. When we encounter problems and rely on God instead of ourselves, we access his power.

The turning point in our journey through brokenness comes when we stop trying to control the pain and move to a posture of dependence. Breakthrough comes when we turn to God for help.

By taking us to a place of suffering and brokenness, we see what's broken and doesn't work in our lives. A good kingdom journey will take us where we have no place of comfort to retreat. If we set out to make the journey a learning experience, we will discover how God reveals himself through life, no matter how painful it may seem.

PICKING FLAWED PEOPLE

Jesus is in the business of establishing his kingdom on earth and using us to do it. God met Marisa halfway through her kingdom journey in the person of a twelve-year-old boy. He used Allan to teach Marisa dependence. He used Marisa to bring his kingdom to Allan. Allan's story later brought hope to many others like the woman at the clinic. This is the ripple effect of a kingdom that is not of this world. As we allow God to use us, he multiplies our efforts, which flow from one person to another.

If you're like me, you're perpetually tempted to build God's kingdom on your own strength and resources; however,

Jesus' discipleship program didn't allow for self-reliance. He gave his followers assignments to accomplish. Lest there be any confusion about whose power they were depending on, he gave them no resources. Instead, they had to depend on God for everything, even their most basic physical needs. Kingdom journey was the great instructor. God used it to transform the disciples from self-trusting people to God-trusting people.

Day by day, moment-by-moment, the disciples learned to depend on God. As he provided for them, they learned to trust him more. Jesus constantly pointed out when he saw faith in people. This was his method to build faith in his disciples.

If I had been one of Jesus' disciples, one of questions I would have had is, "Why me? Why did you pick me when there were thousands of others who were more qualified, more talented, more worthy?"

This is a question I wrestle with even now. It's a question that I have when I look at the characters of the Bible, too. All of them were tremendously flawed. Noah was a drunk, yet his faith led God to pardon the human race from extinction. Sarah's faith was so weak that when God said he was going to use her, she laughed. Lot was incestuous, but from his lineage came David, and thus, Jesus. Judah slept with a prostitute and then condemned his daughter-in-law for engaging in prostitution — with him! Yet, his name became the name of a kingdom. Moses was so afraid of public speaking that he denied God's call twice, but the Lord used him to save a nation. David was an adulterous murderer, but he led Israel into its Golden Age. The list of people who were unworthy of God's favor goes on and on; yet, he used them all to do extraordinary things.

Why doesn't God use more-qualified people? Why does he choose his servants from a crowd of broken, flawed, sinful men, and women? Perhaps, because brokenness is all he has to work with. Perhaps it's to encourage the rest of us who know our own flaws all too well. Whatever the reason, we know this for sure: God's kingdom shines most brightly through the undesirables.

Before bringing Allan to Meshack's home, Marisa brought him to her team's house. She made him a sandwich and sat him on the couch to watch a movie. Meshack showed him how to use the bathroom — he'd never seen a toilet before. Allan fell asleep on the couch.

As she listened to him snore, Marisa prayed. "God, if you were to ask me to pick one out and bring him home, I wouldn't have picked Allan. I would have picked the five-year-old that followed us out of the church to the bus stop because he was determined to go with us. You chose Allan, and where there was no way, you did it. I'm in awe of you. When you picked me out, did you pick me like this?"

This is what we learn when we have to depend completely upon God. We come to the end of ourselves and come to rely on the God who is so far beyond ourselves.

In so doing, we take another important step toward realizing the goal of trusting God with our lives.

CHAPTER 10 NOTES

47. Quoted in BrainyQuote.com, *David Brainerd Quotes*, http://www.brainyquote.com/quotes/authors/d/david_brainerd.html.

48. Jerry Bridges and Bob Bevington, *The Bookends of the Christian Life*, (Wheaton, IL: Crossway Books, 2009), 124.

CHAPTER 11: THE PURPOSES OF POVERTY

Poverty is the schoolmaster of character. — Antiphanes[49]

I remember as a young boy walking with my mom through New York City. A man seated on the sidewalk caught my attention. He had a sign that read, "I am blind and deaf and I have no legs. Please help me."

In front of the man was a cup. It hit me like a punch to the gut. I wanted to cry. Somehow up to that point, I'd been insulated from the world's pain. "Mom, how can that be? Why can't he hear or see? What should we do?" The memory of that man haunted me for days.

As a teenager on my kingdom journey to Peru, I felt a similar sensation as our bus prepared to ascend the Andes Mountains. It was dusk and we were stalled in a remote region waiting for some bulldozers to move dirt and boulders from the road. As I looked out the window, I noticed a Peruvian woman and her two small children sitting on the side of the road.

"What are they doing out here so far from civilization?" I thought. "They have no place to stay tonight, no one to help them." Something inside me wanted to reach out and care for them, but I didn't have a clue what to do. I felt powerless.

The brokenness we experience on a journey is the raw material God uses to establish his kingdom in us. After he heals our wounds, he uses that healing experience to heal others. I wrote earlier about how Erin's harrowing rape eventually led to liberating an entire classroom of Kenyan girls, many of whom had been assaulted themselves. And how Mike's physical brokenness on the beach allowed his whole community to realize that they, too, were broken. Our brokenness allows others around us to see their own brokenness and move beyond it to a place of healing.

This is what the Body of Christ is meant to be — broken, just as Jesus was for the world. This is how church happens. *We connect to one another through our poverty.*

We begin our journey focused on ourselves, but it is not for us. We are on a pilgrimage, yes, but ultimately it is a pilgrimage to identify with the world's brokenness.

Jesus began his journey by quoting Isaiah 61, "He has anointed me to preach good news to the poor. He has sent me to proclaim freedom for the prisoners and recovery of sight for the blind, to release the oppressed." We do as our Lord did by identifying with the poor, the sick, the imprisoned, and the lost.

We may begin our pilgrimage with noble aspirations of how we will bring something to the poor. But, inevitably, we must allow God to first heal what is sick and poor inside our own souls. Then, he can use us in the world. If it is a pilgrimage to the poor on which we embark, we must first discover our own poverty. Whenever you visit *them*, says Jesus in Matthew 25, you visit *him* (Matthew 25:34-45). Ultimately, our pilgrimage is to the poor because in them we see Jesus and find the kingdom.

When we encounter the poor in a meaningful way, what had been a journey about us begins to reveal itself as a kingdom journey. This is what Nic Schlagman, with the African Refugee Development Center (ARDC), discovered in Tel Aviv.

Nic usually finds homeless refugees living in Levinsky Park. They are mostly from the Darfur region of Sudan where they face a tribal war that has killed 400,000 and displaced millions of individuals. Many, however, come from other parts of East Africa, including a growing Eritrean population.[50]

The refugees' journey to Israel is harrowing. Refugees pay smugglers exorbitant sums to traffic them through the dangerous East African deserts. During this passage, many die of heat stroke, dehydration, starvation, or fatigue. Next, they have to travel through Egypt's menacing Sinai Desert; the same desert through which the Hebrews fled from Egypt thousands of years ago. Along the way, they face the constant danger of the Egyptian military, whose policy is to shoot on sight. The women are regularly raped by smugglers.

The Eritrean refugees flee to Israel because they believe that they will be treated with dignity by a people who understand persecution. In that sense, they leave with the same aspirations we have when we set out on a kingdom journey. We hope we'll be welcomed when we arrive as strangers in a new place.

On a kingdom journey, we become foreigners in another land, sojourners in another culture. In the same way that the African refugees are marginalized, so are those of us who leave on a journey. We lose our social status and any sense of ownership, exchanging it all for an opportunity…a rumor of freedom. We live in the margins. In a sense, we are poor. At the least, we are more likely to encounter our own poverty.

There are always uncomfortable moments when you go into a culture that is not your own: misunderstandings, muggings, sickness, strange foods, extreme weather, lack of air conditioning or instant coffee; and more…or less. All of these factors combine to make life more difficult for the traveler. We go on a kingdom journey and begin to have some small understanding of what life is like for the marginalized.

God associates with people living in the margins. He tells the rich how difficult it will be for them. When we're poor, we recognize our need for God. That need moves us into dependence and our trust relationship deepens.

The Jews of the Old Testament lived at the margins, expelled from their land again and again — forced to live as foreigners in other nations. Just like the Eritreans, God made them live as refugees. Abraham lived in Canaan, Lot in Sodom, Jacob and his sons in Egypt. When Israel and Judah were conquered, they were exiled to Assyria and Babylon. After the second temple was destroyed in the first century, the Jews were scattered. They were forced to live everywhere, including Europe, where they were persecuted viciously — the most extreme incident being the Holocaust.

Nic and ARDC are learning from history. He says, "If this land doesn't allow us to flower from the experiences of our history as wanderers for 2000 years, then what have we learned?"[51]

Nic first noticed the refugees when he was walking around one of the seedier neighborhoods of Tel Aviv. Eventually, his concern for them grew to the point that he started working with ARDC to help provide for the refugees' basic needs. Nic wanted to help them become comfortable in Israeli culture.

Taking us to the margins of life where we can discover poverty, God wants us to see ourselves in those who are poor. He wants us to identify with people who are outcasts, estranged from the comforts of home and community.

The Bible specifically commands us to take care of the foreigners and wanderers amongst us. We, who are strangers and sojourners on this planet, have a basis for associating with them. "Do not deprive the foreigner or the fatherless of justice," says God in Deuteronomy. "Remember that you were slaves in Egypt and the LORD your God redeemed you from there. That is why I command you to do this," (Deuteronomy 24:17-18).

Scripture is full of accounts of and commands for God's people to take care of the poor. Deuteronomy 24, for example, commands farmers to leave some of their produce in the fields so that "foreigners, the fatherless, and widows" can gather it for food, something Boaz allowed Ruth to do. "Do not oppress a foreigner," says Exodus 23:9, "you yourselves know how it feels to be foreigners, because you were foreigners in Egypt." Leviticus 19:33 states, "The foreigner residing among you must be treated as your native-born. Love them as yourself, for you were foreigners in Egypt."

God has been sending his people out on kingdom journeys since Adam and Eve left the garden. God told them to leave home, abandon all, and go to the desolate, broken places on earth. He does this so they can experience their own poverty. In sending the entire nation out from Egypt, he allowed them to experience abandon, brokenness, and dependence — all that before abundance.

God has always used kingdom journey as a spiritual discipline — a resource to build compassion, a means of changing hearts toward the marginalized in our society, a way to direct our minds toward his kingdom. In each new generation, as he uses this tool afresh, the people of God are awakened, opening their hearts to the poor, the oppressed, and the marginalized.

Once at the ARDC shelter, the Jewish volunteers were discussing their plans for Passover. The refugees staying at the shelter asked questions as their interest grew in the Seder ritual that Jews celebrate every Passover. "As we explained the festival," Nic said, "it occurred to me that this wasn't just our story, this was really the refugees' story. They literally, in many cases, walked through Egypt, crossing the Sinai, to flee oppression, hoping to find freedom. We had this idea that we would try to create this Seder together."[52]

They hosted the Seder in Levinsky Park, the area where Nic first saw the refugees hanging around, aimless and poor. The Passover meal was served with a thousand people attending; a mix of refugees, curious Israelis, and volunteers. A choir from a refugee church came and sang traditional Passover songs.

One Israeli woman at the event met a man named, Johannes. She asked, "Why did you come to Israel, not some other developed nation?"

Johannes' reply touched her heart: "We came to Israel, a place of miracles, and we seek help from you — people who understand our misery. I came through the way that Moses and his people, your people, crossed. Help us! Please, help us get out of this suffering."[53]

Kingdom journey makes us like Johannes. It allows us to enter into the stories of the Bible. To walk as Moses and his people walked. We journey to the Promised Land with Abraham. We experience the life of Jesus and his disciples, who wandered the land of Israel with no place to lay their heads. It makes us homeless as they were homeless. It allows us to find our homes in the kingdom of God where we will always have a home. It turns our eyes from ourselves to the "least of these."

In the kingdom of God, those who are downtrodden in the world are called the greatest in heaven. It's a paradox that turns our assumptions on their heads. Henri Nouwen says it like this:

> "Those who are marginal in the world are central in the church, and that is how it is supposed to be! Thus, we are called as members of the church to keep going to the margins of our society. The homeless, the starving, parentless children, people with AIDS, our emotionally disturbed brothers and sisters — they require our first attention. The church will always be renewed when our attention shifts from ourselves to those who need our care. The blessing of Jesus always comes to us through the poor. The most remarkable experience of those who work with the poor is that, in the end, the poor give more than they receive. They give food to us."[54]

When we claim our own poverty and brokenness — and we connect them with the poverty of the world — we become the church of the broken. This is the church where Jesus, who was first broken, is most visible.

Community and vulnerability are essential for the church of the broken. We must authentically share both our pain and joy. As one body, we will deeply experience one another's hurts, as well as their honor. As Paul says, "If one part suffers, every part suffers with it; if one part is honored, every part rejoices with it" (1 Corinthians 12:26).

We might rather not be part of this broken body. Every time we love others deeply, we become vulnerable and feel their pain profoundly. However, without vulnerability, there can be no joy. Joy is hidden in the pain. When we share the pain we stretch our capacity to also share the joy.

Bono, lead singer of the rock band, U2, reflected on some of the same themes in his speech at the National Prayer Breakfast in 2006. President George W. Bush and others of the nation's elite were in attendance when the rock-star-turned-prophet said:

> "God is in the slums, in the cardboard boxes where the poor play house. God is in the silence of a mother who has infected her child with a virus that will end both their lives... God is in the cries heard under the rubble of war... God is in the debris of wasted opportunity and lives, and God is with us if we are with them."[55]

It's not a coincidence that poverty is mentioned more than two thousand times in the Scriptures. For too long some of us have been asking God to bless what we're doing, rather than asking him to show us what he's already blessing. Our kingdom journey should take us to the poor. When we arrive in that place where they are, we will realize we didn't bring

KINGDOM JOURNEYS: REDISCOVERING THE LOST SPIRITUAL DISCIPLINE

the kingdom to them. In fact, we found it in their midst.

COMPASSION AND AMBIGUITY

This is not simple. Layers of ambiguity can cloud our interactions with people who are poor. When we peel back the layers of our own poverty, we expose mixed motives.

When a beggar girl greeted my bus in India with her hands outstretched, asking for help for the baby on her hip, a voice inside me whispered, "What are you going to do about it?" I've got money in my pocket, but I know it won't solve her problem. I think, "When it is spent, then what?" If I give her money and she buys food, then at least her hunger pains will stop for a while. On the other hand, what if it's a scam as so often is the case? How can I know she will use the money as she should?

You want to help the needy ones, but giving to beggars can be complicated. Anyone who saw the movie, *Slumdog Millionaire*, understands it can be a racket. Won't I just be increasing her dependency if I give her a handout? Giving her money could do more harm than good.

I can't know for sure. It's immobilizing. Besides, all I've got is dollars. I'd have to get out of the bus in the rain. I'm sleepy too. I can't just do nothing. I'm an American. We are the richest people in the world.

We know "to whom much is given, much is expected." We labor under the guilt of our abundance. In that moment, paralyzed by ambiguity, uncomfortable that people are grabbing for my wallet, I do nothing. Called to a lifestyle of giving, of activism, I risk becoming a parody of myself, maybe even like Peter, who when he saw Christ, denied him.

I guess the best defense against this predicament is to simply stay away from such ambiguous situations. Getting involved is messy. Better to turn the channel, better to get distracted by the clutter and noise of my own life. Better to not have to walk away in the first place. All of which is why I, like you, need the discipline of a kingdom journey.

PRAYING FOR GRACE

There was another beggar woman who caught my attention in India. It looked like another dip into ambiguity. I wanted to run. But Grace came to me that evening in Hyderabad.

We'd been accosted by beggars everywhere we went. My spirit felt bruised by it all. It was a long day, and I was ready to retreat to a safe place. Then, walking to our last meeting, I heard behind me, "Sir, sir!"

I recoiled inside, guarded myself, and looked to see a small woman beckoning me. I silently wondered how to fend her off.

"Sir, I have cancer. Mommy, Daddy dead. I need to catch train. Help me!"

"Right," I thought. There was no grace in me.

I listened as she shared more details of her plight. I asked her to come to where we could talk inside the building. I promised to help somehow. She agreed to walk with us.

Once she was inside, I asked Raju to translate, so she could speak in Hindi. She was skin and bones. She showed us a big lump on her neck — an enlarged thyroid. She showed us her deformed arm. She showed us her medical records.

"I think she is telling you the truth," said Raju.

"What is your name?" I asked.

"It is Grace," she answered.

We gathered some of the nearby team members. Noe prayed a powerful prayer. He declared, "Grace, God says you are beautiful! You are beautiful."

She was crying. You could feel God's presence. A wave of emotion hit me.

We sent her away with money for the train and for medicines, and we sent her with hugs. If she found grace through us in that short interaction, after a day of searching for it, we found that grace is also a person's name.

We hear about grace in church as an abstraction. That night she took on human form and kissed our spirits. She walked away in the night, but the spirit of Grace lingered with us. I was better for it.

I was lucky that Grace came to me that day. However, I still had to leave my home. I still had to go to meet her. I had to journey halfway around the world and immerse myself in the discomfort of poverty.

In all my travels, I've found that this often is the case. God uses physical poverty to reveal our own spiritual poverty and to help us join him in healing the whole world.

If we are willing to step into the dirty dark areas of the world — where hope is in short supply — God's grace will always meet us there.

CHAPTER 11 NOTES

49. Quoted in BrainyQuote.com, *Antiphanes Quotes,* http://www.brainyquote.com/quotes/authors/a/antiphanes.html.

50. Adam Chandler, "For Refugees, a Modern Exodus," *InTheMoment,* http://momentmagazine.wordpress.com/2011/01/06/for-refugees-a-modern-exodus/.

51. Ibid.

52. Ibid.

53. Tamar Orvell, "In Tel Aviv: The Orange on the Passover Seder Plate," *Only Connect: A dual citizen's wide-angle lens, dispersing dots of light,* http://www.only-connect.blogspot.com/2009/04/om-tel-aviv-orange-on-passover-seder.html.

54. Henri Nouwen, *Bread for the Journey,* 320.

55. Quoted in "Transcript: Bono remarks at the National Prayer Breakfast," *USA Today,* http://www.usatoday.com news/washington/2006-02-02-bono-transcript_x.htm.

CHAPTER 11: YOUR OWN KINGDOM JOURNEY

"In the year that somebody you loved died, you go into the temple, if that is your taste, or you hide your face in the little padded temple of your hands, and a voice says, 'Whom shall I send into the pain of a world where people die?' If you are not careful, you may find yourself answering, 'Send me.' You may hear the voice say, 'Go.' Just go." — Frederick Buechner[56]

I first met Joe Bunting in Santa Barbara. One day, he read one of my blog posts entitled, "How do I know what to do with my life?" He had been asking this same question and the blog provoked him to do something. He sensed that I might have the answer he needed. So he emailed, "I got a sudden urge to get up, leave work, and start walking to Georgia. That's not from God, right? What if it is?"

What if it was, indeed.

It's no wonder Joe was having an encounter with

restlessness. He had graduated from college about a year before and was working a desk job as an administrative assistant. He called himself a "professional coffee maker." His potential was barely being tapped. He was struggling to break out of the status quo. But because the job paid well, and he had student loans to pay off, Joe stayed where he was. As much as Joe found his job unfulfilling, he needed it.

What would you have suggested to Joe? Would you have told him to just go? Or would you have told him not to be flaky? It's one thing to be struck by the Gift of Restlessness — it's another to know what to do with it.

My friend and teacher, Andrew Shearman, probably did more to help me wake up to the kingdom of God than any other man. I heard Andrew preach at our church in 1992 and instantly fell in love with his message. We became friends and started talking about what it means to follow Jesus.

Now, when Andrew and I get together, we have conversations until well past midnight. We wake up groggy, stumble to the coffee maker, and continue where we left off. Andrew weaves dreams and magnificent faith stories through his conversations. He says when the disciples saw Jesus coming, their hearts supernaturally leapt within them. They dropped everything and left for the kingdom journey Jesus was calling them on. But I see it another way.

The different perspectives arise from the two very distinct pictures of Peter's calling we see in Matthew 4 and Luke 5. Andrew likes Matthew's version. In it, Jesus is walking along the Sea of Galilee when he sees Peter and his brother, Andrew, fishing.

"Come follow me," says Jesus. "I send you out to fish for people" (Matthew 4:19). At once, the brothers leave their nets and follow Christ. This is the kind of hearts-leaping-to-abandonment experience that Andrew loves.

In Luke's gospel, however, Jesus traveled throughout Galilee as an itinerant preacher. Along the way, he met Peter, who said that his mother-in-law was very sick. Jesus agreed to visit and heal her. When Jesus entered Peter's humble house, he bent over Peter's mother-in-law and rebuked the fever. Immediately, it left her, and she became well. Soon, word spread. That evening, the sick came from every direction to Peter's house to be healed.

After he healed every sick and harassed one in the village, Jesus left to continue his tour of Galilee. He appeared at Lake Gennesaret and began to preach. The crowd was huge and there was no good place to address them. What should he do? He looked around for a solution, and then saw his friend, Peter, washing his net beside his boat. Jesus asked to use his boat to preach. Of course, Peter agreed. After Jesus finished preaching, he and Peter rowed out into the lake.

"Put out into the deep water, and let down the nets for a catch," Jesus says.

"Master, we've worked hard all night and haven't caught anything," says Peter. "But because you say so, I will let down the nets" (Luke 5:4-5). Peter has seen what Jesus can do. Peter has reason to believe that something special is about to happen. When Peter begins to pull the net back up, it is so heavy that he has to wrestle it up. The net begins to break. There are so many fish that they fill up two boats until they begin to sink.

When they arrive at the shore, Peter falls at Jesus' feet. "Go away from me, Lord. I am a sinful man!" he cries. But Jesus lifts him to his feet.

"Don't be afraid. From now on you will catch men," Jesus says (Luke 5:8-11). Peter and his fishing partners, James and

John, then leave everything to follow Jesus.

These are two very different stories. Andrew likes Matthew's story because it features Peter's passion and intuitive understanding of who Jesus is. I prefer Luke's version with its more gradual relationship-building process. Both are in the Bible. The question is which path should Joe have taken? Matthew's or Luke's? If he had followed Matthew, he would have left immediately without telling anyone, and set out for Georgia. Had he followed Luke's model, Joe would take several months of waiting and watching before he made his journey.

For Joe, the question was whether or not he was correctly discerning God's call to a kingdom journey. My advice to him was that hearing God can be a hard habit to start. If we're ever going to learn to hear God, we have to give him the benefit of the doubt. Since Jesus already commanded his disciples to go out into the nations, our posture should be one of leaning forward, assuming that Luke 10 applies to us, too. At the same time, we should seek confirmation from other believers who hear the voice of God, that's always wise.

Joe didn't quit his job and start hitchhiking to Georgia that day, but the seed of kingdom journey was planted in his soul. A few months later, he came to a conference that our organization hosted in Georgia. Several months after that, Joe left for a year-long trip around the world knowing he was finally following God's call.

Joe was right when he e-mailed me. He sensed the Gift of Restlessness — God's call to leave everything. Mirroring the path we see in Luke's version, however, he had to get more confirmation.

Some people take a path that looks more like Matthew's version. On May 19, 2009, Dan Snyder worked as a detective in Denver, Colorado. Three days later, he boarded a plane that would take him to a training camp for a year-long mission trip. Unlike Joe's slow-testing process, Dan's story began abruptly. He felt the Gift of Restlessness rising up to a bursting point and he left.

As you consider going on a kingdom journey, which path will you take? If you see restlessness for the gift it is, then I recommend you lean forward. Yes, there are obligations and responsibilities — debt, and commitments and duties you need to honor. But don't allow yourself to be locked down by other people's expectations of you.

We all need a journey to grow, especially when we're still young and before we're locked into the straightjacket of mortgage payments and kids in school. Far from being a flaky shirking of responsibility, a kingdom journey is often exactly the right step.

THE BICYCLE PRINCIPLE

The real question we need to ask is, "Am I called? Do I feel God pulling me to a kingdom journey?" If the answer is yes, then begin moving forward.

If God is not in it, he will stop you. You will feel it. It will be hard to ignore. Part of your journey involves facing the obstacles that block your way. These obstacles make you ask, "Did God really call me to this?" They're inevitable and can be discouraging. This is why learning to hear the Lord's voice is so important.

Discovering your calling is like riding a bicycle. You have to get it moving to steer it. If the bike isn't moving, when you turn the handles and lean your weight into a turn, you won't change directions, you'll just fall over. In fact, you can only turn a bike when it is moving.

God won't steer us if we've not followed his guidance and started moving. Joe had a difficult time discerning the Lord's voice because he wasn't moving. He was trapped in his safe, comfortable job — wanting to leave but afraid to do so.

If you feel like Joe, I recommend you do two things. First, pray. Then, get in motion. What God asks you to do may seem risky, but you can start small. For example, think about going on a practice kingdom journey over the weekend. Anyone can do that.

God cares about people and wants to touch them. Jesus' heart burst with compassion when he surveyed the crowds of needy people. The best way to start moving is to reach out to the poor, the oppressed, and the hungry *wherever you are.*

In Isaiah 58:10, God says, "If you'll spend yourself on behalf of the hungry and satisfy the needs of the oppressed, then the Lord will guide you always." If we reach out to those whose needs outweigh our own, he will lead us.

You may wonder how God will help you take on what seem like impossible tasks. He promises us what we hunger for most — a direct connection to himself, a hotline to God, will be established. Again in Isaiah 58:9, he says, "Then you will call, and the Lord will answer, you will cry for help and he will say: 'Here I am.'"

Many of us want provision and connection without sacrifice. We want to be blessed with God's guidance when we're not moving. However, only those in motion need guidance. By focusing on our own needs, we are dead in the water. We become self-absorbed and cut off from any divine direction. Only as we make God's agenda our priority do we begin to get the big picture of our life.

God's guidance takes on many forms. Once Paul began to move, he was guided by circumstances, dreams, visions, the counsel of others, and Scripture. God does not tell us how he will guide us. He simply says that if we'll be about his business, he will guide us.

Compare this to how we normally look for direction. If you're like me, you'll weigh the pros and cons; seeking the option that benefits you the most. Maybe one reason we have difficulty discerning God's will is that we have ignored it for so long. He wants us to reach out to people when we may prefer to play it safe. Isaiah 58 doesn't say, "If you'll do just the basics and look out for your own needs, then I'll guide you." Instead, he calls us to the poor — the slum, the trash heap — and promises to show us the way home.

HOW DO I START MY OWN KINGDOM JOURNEY?

To apply the principles of Luke 10, you have to choose the "foolhardy" path of dependence upon God. Be forewarned if you do, you're no longer in control. It's a choice full of risks, one that will result in surprises and adventures.

For example, consider the experience of Chad Mast and Chris Telfer. They decided to test the limits of the Luke 10 protocol in Tibet in 2007. God had proved himself faithful in the Bible. They decided to trust him in the same way that the disciples did and take absolutely nothing on a journey.

Chad describes what happened as they tried to read and follow Jesus' instructions:

> "We took that to mean not to take tents or food. Our contact had asked us to prayer walk through some local towns. The town we

were in was about as remote as you get. Our previous two camping trips consisted of 15-30 degree weather with the occasional snowflake.

We set out on our adventure and asked the Lord to go before us and open the doors that he wanted for us. We arrived in the town and a little child stood before us, near his father."

Chad and Chris followed the boy and sat next to a group of local men who spoke a Tibetan dialect. Chad took out his Bible and began reading Luke 10. He told the group they were looking for the "man of peace" in town.

Before they knew it, they were befriended by the group of men. As Chad explains, "We were on the back of their motorcycles riding through the mountains of China… we had no idea what we were doing or where we were going."

They eventually pulled up to a house. One of the locals escorted them inside to meet the man's parents. Chad and Chris shook the hands with the man and put their stuff down in an open room of the house. "We couldn't believe what was happening," Chad recalls.

After they stored their gear, their new friends asked Chad and Chris to come pray with them at the temple. They gladly accepted. Everyone traveled through the valley and across a stream to a local Buddhist monastery. When they arrived, the doors were locked. Their friends gestured that no one could enter.

Then, two monks with keys walked up and guided the group through the monastery. Throughout their adventure, Chad and Chris prayed and worshiped. From there, the Tibetan men took the two Americans up on a mountain ridge that overlooked the entire valley. Standing at an elevation of about 12,000 feet, surrounded by huge, mountainous peaks, Chad and Chris smiled at the adventure they were having.

When everyone returned to the house, they sat around a stove, drinking tea and eating soup. They conversed through charades and limited Chinese.

When dinner was over, one of the Tibetans began to play music on a small guitar. After he finished, he gave the guitar to Chris, who played a worship song. The Tibetans shouted with joy and everyone danced around the room. Again, Chad remembers, "We couldn't believe what was happening."

After worshiping, their new friends insisted on giving Chad and Chris a heated bed with huge blankets covering every side. They laughed with the Tibetans before going to sleep.

Chad took out his Bible and read Luke 10 again. "We found out that the Lord had provided most of what the disciples experienced," Chad said.

In the morning, they ate breakfast, laughing as they drank yak milk with their hosts. After finishing, they decided to climb the mountain peak and thank the Lord for what he had done. At the top, Chad stood and proclaimed the freedom of Jesus Christ over the valley.

"I stood with my arms outstretched," Chad said, "thanking the Lord for the life that I live. I realized that I was born for a radical life. I was born to set captives free from the bondages of the world. I realized how madly in love I was with the Creator of the World. I realized that my life was Luke 10, and I never wanted it to be any different."

This is the point of a kingdom journey: to learn that life, itself, can be filled with such radical dependence on God that you will never want to return to a "normal" life ever again. You will be *wrecked for the ordinary.*

ASSIGNMENTS THAT BECOME JOURNEYS

Sometimes we receive an assignment in life that catches us by surprise and turns into a kingdom journey. Military deployment can sometimes be that way.

Jen Schwab was sent to Afghanistan with the Army. She later came to view her deployment as a kingdom journey. "I had gotten to a place in my life where I realized I had no clue what I was doing," she said. "Many aspects of my life were a mess, and I had finally acknowledged to God that I did not have it all together. Then I got the call to deploy."

Jen knew there was going to be something special about this voyage. "I knew it was a call to greatness in my life," she remembered." I remember climbing the steps of that plane, just tingling all over, knowing that the Jen who would get on that plane would never come back."

Jen thought she could find her identity in dodging bullets and sleeping in the dirt. She was drawn to adventure. When she arrived in Afghanistan, she was issued a mattress and mini-fridge. "My hardest challenges," she said, "came from the people I lived with. I had a lot of not-so-proud moments in that year."

In the midst of this, Jen encountered Jesus. She was broken for hurting people — both fellow soldiers and her Afghan friends. Her breaking wasn't easy; when her friends confronted her about selfish behavior, it hurt.

The whole experience wrecked Jen. It took her years to process what she had learned while deployed. "But," she says, "I knew when I left Afghanistan that I could never be the same. God used that year to give me the kingdom perspective he'd always wanted me to have."

DEALING WITH WET BLANKETS

One area that can be difficult to navigate is how to respond when an authority figure tells you, "Don't go." An authority — sometimes a concerned parent — may even say your call is not from God. During times like this, it is especially important to discern what to do.

When Andrew Maas first considered a kingdom journey, authority figures in his life discouraged him. It caused him to delay his journey for years. No doubt they had the best of intentions. Parents want their kids to get good jobs and live secure lives. They want them to be responsible. People who have been burned by life want to help impetuous young people avoid pain. But that raises a difficult issue: If God said, "Go!" If he issues a "Deploy" order, and the people around you are throwing wet blankets on you, what do you do? What do you do if the most important people in your life aren't supportive?

LESSONS FROM CAMBODIA

In 1979, Pol Pot's regime was ending. His reign of terror left two million of his own people dead. Those Cambodians who could escape fled through the jungles to refugee camps along the Thai border.

At the time, I was a senior at Wheaton College. When I read about the Cambodian crisis, something stirred in my spirit. I was seized by a sense of revulsion at the way the people were suffering and I knew something had to be done. I sensed I needed to go and help some of the hundreds of thousands of refugees spilling across the border. It would require a journey, an uprooting of my life to a violent and pain-wracked part of the world. But I had to go.

From the beginning, there were obstacles. First, I was in love with the woman who would become my wife. Karen and I had been dating for almost a year and leaving her in the midst of our courtship was going to be heart-rending. On top of that, I would be leaving in the middle of my senior year of college. I would have to convince my professors to allow me to take independent studies in order to graduate on time. I also needed a sponsoring agency.

I found an agency called Food for the Hungry that was looking for workers and I applied for a position. I sensed God was in it and was confident I would soon be serving in Cambodia.

Then my train of destiny derailed. Food for the Hungry rejected my application.

I was crushed. I knew I was qualified. I had traveled extensively and had been on short-term mission trips before. I had the drive and determination. Why couldn't they see it? It felt so frustrating. I scrambled back to the Lord.

"God," I prayed. "I am willing to give up time with Karen. I'm willing to give up a huge chunk of my senior year. I'm willing to sacrifice all of this to serve your dream. Help me, Lord. Just get me on that plane."

A few days later, I received a call from Food for the Hungry. "We can take two more people than we thought," said the representative, "and you're one of them."

I couldn't believe it. It was a miracle! But now I had a new obstacle: time.

The plane to Cambodia was leaving in three weeks. I didn't have long to negotiate with my professors about the courses I would miss. Also, there was an issue with finances: I had to raise money to go on the trip.

When I shared about the trip with my closest group of supporters, they had major red flags. In the end, they didn't believe God was in it. They said I shouldn't go.

For me, it became a question of obeying what God was saying or listening to the opinions of people. I didn't have the money and I didn't have the backing of a support team. But I had to make a decision. Should I go without confirmation, without support, and without enough money? Or should I play it safe?

On faith, I committed, trusting that God would provide the funds and change my supporters' hearts.

At the last second, everything fell into place. The icing on the cake came when I was at the airport and received a phone call. My supporters had changed their minds. They saw that God was in it and committed to covering the cost of my trip. I joined the other eleven participants on the airplane and was off on a new kingdom journey. We flew in a 747 that had been reserved to fly refugees back to the U.S. It was completely empty except for our group and a few attendants. I stretched out over four seats and went to sleep.

PLANNING YOUR OWN KINGDOM JOURNEY

Benny Veale wanted to plan his own kingdom journey. He had been on a preplanned one in 2008, but he needed more. He wanted to do something that wasn't organized by someone else. In 2010, Benny began planning his very own kingdom journey.

His first step was to recruit Miles, a fellow traveler he had journeyed with, to co-lead the trip. Miles was a logical choice for Benny to team with. In the past, they had dreamed about it while sitting around campfires and watching stars.

First, they had to decide on a destination. They prayed and sensed a leading to Nepal, a tiny country tucked in the Himalayas. Neither had been there before, but they felt something calling out to them from that remote nation.

India borders Nepal, so it seemed like a logical place to start. They had also initially planned to go to northern Thailand to work with a known contact there. However, they realized the only way to get from Thailand to India would be to fly, and because of the added costs, they rejected the idea. They would keep it simple: India and Nepal.

Next, they started recruiting people to go. Benny already had people in mind to ask; men whom he had taken under his wing at some point. Miles had a list of people, too. Soon there were a dozen guys interested in the journey. As Miles and Benny worked on the logistics of the trip, people began to drop out. Some said they no longer felt called and others couldn't get released from commitments they'd made. The dozen finally dwindled down to two others sojourners. However, Miles and Benny were happy. "We didn't want a bunch of half-committed people. We wanted men who were ready to go to brokenness and back," Benny said.

The group funded the trip with savings and fundraising. Their support-raising style was a little unorthodox. They never asked for money. They depended on God to lead people to them who felt called to give. Their goal was $4,000 per person. By the time they had to buy their plane tickets a few months before they were set to leave, however, they had only raised about $100. Still, they took the leap of faith and bought the tickets on credit. Their faith was rewarded.

By the time they left, they had raised about $9,000 of their $16,000 goal, and the money continued to come in during their travels.

Beyond getting the requisite travel visas and vaccinations, Benny and Miles made very few plans. Their goal was to seek the Lord throughout their trip and listen for God's itinerary. They did contact one person, an Indian man who led a ministry in Dehradun, and planned to spend time serving with him. Everything else, they would let God decide.

As you consider going on a kingdom journey, there are two paths you can take. The first is to design your own journey. This is labor-intensive. Depending on where you want to go, it could take months to prepare. There are dozens of details to consider: visas, vaccines, travel methods, lodging, etc. Some of this you can do on the fly, but your pre-journey preparation will still take longer than you think. For example, because he was in the United States the whole time, Andrew's biking journey required minimal supplies. The journey lasted less than a month and didn't take long to prepare. Benny and Miles' four-month journey, however, took more than six months to prepare.

MENTORS, MINISTRY, AND MONEY

If you feel God calling you to craft your own journey, you'll want to get advice from someone who has gone before. When I went on my first kingdom journey, I didn't have anyone to help me better understand the inner journey. You can't avoid all the mistakes I made, but you can be better prepared to deal with them if you take the time to learn what to expect in advance.

The goal of kingdom journey is to get to a place where you're so out of your own control that you can experience brokenness and wrestle with fundamental issues of identity and purpose.

A mentor or coach will offer perspective, encourage you to "tough it out" during the hard times, and hold your feet to the fire when necessary. At some point you may find yourself on a train in India, at a dirty hostel in Cambodia, or in a mud hut in South Africa, and you will feel exhausted — ready to take the easy way out. The easy way out, however, will short-circuit the process of moving to brokenness, which leads to dependence.

A kingdom journey is usually more about your own internal growth than the outward good you do. Of course, there is a balance here — you're the primary beneficiary of the journey, but the journey shows that you aren't the center of the universe. What you do — otherwise known as "ministry" — teaches you that others have needs greater than you do. It helps put God in the driver's seat and compels you to go to *him* for answers to your questions and process.

Community is another tool God uses to help us grow. Like ministry, it forces us to consider the needs of others before our own needs. Having a travel partner or a team will bring conflict, but it will also help you get over yourself and teach you to serve.

Of course you'll need to address the issue of finances before going. How will you pay for your journey? You've got a couple of options: you can save up and pay for it yourself or you can raise financial support.

Rolf Potts, author of the book *Vagabonding*, advocates saving money in advance for your trip. He says the work you do to save up is part of the journey itself. [57]

If you're volunteering or doing mission work as part of

your kingdom journey, then raising support is an option. If you do this, it's usually best to place yourself under the authority of a mission organization or at least a mentor who can give your journey oversight and credibility.

WALKING AS JESUS WALKED

For Benny Veale, Miles, and the two guys they led, their journey helped them to better understand the context in which Jesus lived.

"We came in with few plans and attempted to let go of our expectations," Benny told me. "We surrendered jobs, schooling, and everything else for this calling. We had hopes. Our intention was to be willing to be used wherever and whenever…while putting ourselves in situations where we had to trust in God's faithfulness."

They learned how to walk in faith. They learned about freedom. They learned that the company you keep on a journey is more important than the destination. They came to know God's character and asked him to show them their own character.

Benny told me, "This trip helped us understand Jesus' years in ministry. It gave us an opportunity to journey through it."

They didn't need more knowledge, more sermon points to remember, and more insights about theology. They needed to learn how to journey and to abandon themselves completely to God's care.

The same is true for your journey. There may be those who will question or oppose you. You may have to risk more than you want.

If you are obeying God, don't give up. You'll see that even the risks you take are part of the lessons learned on your kingdom journey.

CHAPTER 12 NOTES

56. Frederick Buechner, *Secrets in the Dark: A Life of Sermons*, (New York: HarperCollins, 2006), 36.

57. Rolf Potts, *Vagabonding: An Uncommon Guide to the Art of Long-Term World Travel*, (New York: Villard Books, 2002), 16 — 20.

CHAPTER 13: SMALL SCALE JOURNEYS

"Go. I am sending you as lambs among wolves."
— Jesus (Matthew 10:16)

Jesus was the original radical. He announced the arrival of a kingdom that would stand common sense on its head. Early on, after his disciples saw him heal the sick and rout the enemy, Jesus turned his boys loose on the countryside. They'd seen enough. Now it was time to do what Jesus had done: heal the sick, raise the dead, and declare the kingdom. (The whole great adventure is chronicled in Luke 9 and 10).

That template works in the modern day as well. The closest thing we see to them on a mass scale we call "short-term mission trips" (STMs). Jesus wants to use the same methods in you that he used to equip his disciples for ministry, methods you may find at work in some STMs. The fruit can be as life-changing as it was for the disciples. A well-designed STM adventure can do much to prime your spiritual pump.

Young people around the world yearn for their own Luke 10 experience. They intuitively sense that theology alone is not enough to fill them and that faith must be tested to be real. Jesus changed the world before and he continues to do so as new generations embark on their journeys.

There's nothing safe about a Luke 10 trip. You might leave with empty pockets and no road map. You can expect the same sense of failure that Jesus experienced in his hometown — or Galilee, where he couldn't do many miracles because of the unbelief around him. Jesus told his disciples they'd face all kinds of trouble and maybe even death. Why should we expect anything less?

The world has attempted all manner of variant Luke 10 trips, but we need to get back to the heart of what Jesus intended in the first place. Those of us who organize short-term missions need to be careful that we don't dumb them down by removing the elements of risk and adventure. We need to be careful about turning them into vacations with a purpose, where the focus is really on the vacation.

Jesus' discipleship experiment in shorter kingdom journeys (whether we call them STMs, "mission trips" or "mini-journeys") has become a lucrative worldwide industry. It's an industry that suffers from all the familiar dilutions that organized religion can bring to the purest of endeavors. I've been right in the middle of it and have made my fair share of mistakes as I've sought to bring STMs to the mainstream church. Over the years, the organization I lead, Adventures in Missions, has taken over 100,000 believers on STMs. But I always point people back to Jesus and his original intent in Luke 10.

MISSION TRIPS AS TRAINING IN SPIRITUAL AUTHORITY

One reason Jesus sent his disciples on mini-journeys is that they needed some practical experience in their spiritual formation. Mission trips are a practice field. On a mission trip, we get to practice wielding God's authority at a new level, in a new place, and in the company of strangers with only God as a resource.

To expand your ability to exercise spiritual authority, rather than taking a wild leap into the unknown, it's better to try a series of short trips — small-scale travels into another level. For example, a weekend ministering to the urban poor in a nearby city may be a good place to start. Do that and you may gain the confidence to do the next thing that requires even more faith. We need to take risks to challenge our faith, but if we're to learn from them, they're best taken in a limited timeframe with a chance for debriefing in community afterwards. That way, you review how God used you. You ask: What went right? What were the missed opportunities?

We don't become proficient at anything overnight. On a mini-journey, we change by degrees, as we step out in faith, practicing new ministry skills. Mastery comes through familiarity and practice. A foray into new territory gives us the opportunity to fail and learn from the experience.

It's easy to get stuck in life's ruts — places where we're trapped by past experience, expectations, and relationships. We need to break free. We need to begin looking for ways out of our immobility and recognize how it limits our spiritual imagination. Very often, what works best is a change of scenery. Different surroundings, different people, different ideas cultivate imagination. If something inside you feels stuck and knows there's more, what you might need to do is to go on a journey — even a short one.

Children start life going on mini-journeys of discovery. They approach their first waterfall, first rainbow, and first trip to the aquarium with wonder. Jesus tells us we need to become like little children. Going on a mini-journey can help you do that. Like a child, you will discover how the spiritual world operates in ways that will make your spirit shout, "Wow!"

SHORT-TERM MISSIONS AND IMPACT

Short-term mission trips themselves may vary substantially in their scope and ministry focus. The prayer behind them may range from no prayer to long seasons of fasting and intercession. Trip leaders may have no experience or be lifelong missionaries. Too many STM leaders don't seem to see the relationship between the trips they're leading and what Jesus intended when he sent his disciples out to minister in the villages of Galilee.

Most short-term mission trips don't resemble a Luke 10 experience. Bags get packed to the brim. *No faith is required.* The main activity may be a construction project that allows for limited interaction with local people. It's a start, but Jesus' model was so much more.

The two mission trips I went on in high school were this way. Our project leader in Guatemala was nineteen years old. I studied some Spanish in school, so I was elected to be the translator. Unfortunately, because we worked in a remote camp, we had little opportunity to talk to the Guatemalans. While the trip impacted me, it would be years before I learned the lessons that a Luke 10 trip might have imparted.

There's no escaping the time dimension of an effective kingdom journey. You have to stay away from home long enough for old habits to wither. Abandonment has to feel complete — you have to lose sight of the shore and feel the violent ocean waves rock your helpless little boat.

While great for giving you a taste of the kingdom, anyone can hold their breath for a weeklong mission trip and resist the possibility of life change. Such trips can get you started on a longer journey. They are wonderful for giving you glimpses of a hurting world and the power of God to change it, but you don't really experience the effects of abandonment in such a short time.

JOURNEYING AT MID-LIFE

A kingdom journey that lasts a year or more may be easier for young people, but it's a spiritual discipline that both young and old need. Older people can and should pray about going on such a trip. It's a way to break out of the stagnating routines we so naturally fall into in our culture.

Teri Frana's experience shows what's possible. Teri felt God calling her away from her corporate career. She followed my blog for a couple of years and actively engaged in the community dialogue about how to live a radical faith like the original disciples. She tells her story of what happened next:

> "I wasn't sure WHAT he was calling me to do. I just knew he was asking me to leave my comfort zone. That's when this great adventure started: the adventure to seek, to find, and pursue what I was created to do for the Kingdom of God. But before I could DO what God created me for, I had a lot to learn, a lot to be stripped away, and a lot of humbling. It's been a very interesting, difficult, wild, and wonderful journey, as I've let go of every preconceived notion about what my life was supposed to look like."

But how do you let go when you are still raising two daughters as a single mom, like Teri? She felt God asking her to bring them along for the journey.

By the time they left Des Moines in the summer of 2010, Teri had sold or given away just about everything she owned. She moved into a motor home and drove to Gainesville, Georgia, to our Adventures in Missions main campus. She had no financial backing and no plan other than to follow Luke 10 principles. One of her daughter's teenage friends felt led to join them.

When Teri and the girls arrived, she found part-time work. She and her little team made ends meet in the RV. When winter arrived and the pipes froze, they all wore blankets to stay warm. She sold the RV, and they temporarily moved in with friends.

It wasn't comfortable, but the experience taught Teri that she didn't have to worry so much. Somehow, it all worked out and her confidence in God's provision increased.

"Most people would call me a nut or at least slightly cracked," Teri says, "but, my heart beats for something more than the comfortableplacesI'vebeen.IwantthefaithIreadaboutintheBible. I want to see what God will do in me, through me, and around me, if I let him."

After a year, the fruit that the experiment is bearing is more evident. Her daughter, Leah, says, "Mom, I don't want to waste any more time living for anything else but what God wants right here, right now."

When summer came, Teri and the girls went on the road again as missionaries. They even added a young Nigerian-American woman named, Emy, to their number.

The team loved their newfound freedom as they simplified and trusted God daily. As Emy said, "We're taught to work hard to get stuff so that we can live life. But we lose life in the process. There is more and I'm getting a chance to live it."

David Nelsestuan took another path to go on his journey. David worked at a financial service company when he went on a mission trip to Matamoros, Mexico. The trip changed him forever. David returned again and again, making it his yearly ritual — thirteen years in a row.

One year, David visited the home of a man named Francisco. Francisco's wife, Guadalupe, was friendly. She sent her children to the Vacation Bible School camps David helped run, but Francisco was gruff and rude. He stood in front of his house as if guarding it.

"Why are you here?" he said. "What have you come for? No one does anything for free." When Francisco was around, Guadalupe and the children were clearly intimidated. David didn't stay long.

Each time David was in Matamoros, he visited Francisco. Slowly, Francisco's heart began to change. In 2010, David helped build a needed addition to Francisco's house. As the walls of the home arose, the relational barriers broke down. No longer did Francisco treat David as an outsider. Now, they treated him like family. David's life was changed, too. Even though he was in his late forties, he quit his job and went to seminary. Upon graduation, he became a pastor in Wisconsin.

In 2011, when almost all American traffic into northern Mexico was at a standstill due to drug violence, David and his team were willing to take the risk. When he saw Francisco, he knew the risk he took for his kingdom journey was worth the effort.

As you begin to explore what God may be saying to you through your own journey, you may find he will call you as he called Eric and Jen Peterson. The Petersons joined me on a one-week trip to a ministry in Swaziland that serves food to hundreds of orphans per day. Now, they and their two children live in the village and feed these children. Jen recounts how it started:

"Our first visit to the village of Nsoko, I stepped off of the bus and before I even had both feet on the ground a little girl had literally climbed her way up my legs and into my arms! She was probably around three or four years old and was covered in sweat and dirt. As soon as she was settled in my arms she took my face in both of her hands and positioned it so that we were locked in an eye-to-eye gaze! I was breathless...

In that second, the Father of the Universe reached down, grabbed a hold of my heart and whispered into my soul, 'There you are!' I realized, to the core of my being, that I had traveled across an ocean to a different continent for the express purpose of holding this little girl in my arms. She knew it and I knew it! She didn't wait for me to bend over and pick her up or even notice her standing there in the red dirt lost in the slanting shadows of the African sun. She made the first move and grabbed hold of me."

Maybe you'll be called like Terri Cash. Terri was in her late forties, divorced, with two grown children living on their own, when God called her on a kingdom journey.

Terri left her comfortable lifestyle in the United States and traveled to Peru, Bolivia, and then South Africa. She had to sleep in a tent on a thin pad on the ground for weeks at a time. She regularly walked for miles, carrying all her necessary possessions —sixty pounds worth — on her back. Terri was no twenty-something, and the African heat and long days wore on her. Terri ate food that she had never eaten before, that she hoped she would never eat again. In South Africa, she injured her back, putting her in bed for several days, ruining her plans to go to Malawi.

When people ask her if they should go on a kingdom journey, Terri tells them, "It's the hardest, best, most fun, loneliest, most challenging, scary, crazy thing I've ever done. I regret I waited until I was almost fifty to do it."

Can you go on a kingdom journey if you're over forty? Can you go on a kingdom journey with kids? Can you go on a kingdom journey if you have a career? Those are all great questions. Terri would ask: "Can you afford *not* to go?"

PROGRAMS

The most popular way to go on a kingdom journey is through an established program. Mormons have made the kingdom journey a standard initiation experience for their young people. Everywhere you go around the world, you'll find Mormon missionaries.

The World Race is an eleven-month program that initiates young adults into a lifestyle of following Jesus by living as the early disciples did for a year.

There are other effective programs, too. Of the faith-based journeys offered, Youth with a Mission's Discipleship Training School is perhaps the most established. It's a six-month experience divided into two parts. Initially, students spend three months in the classroom. Then they spend the second half of the program doing outreach internationally.

There are countless other opportunities involving kingdom journey missions and travel. Some people serve full-time missionaries in a country to which they feel called. Others join a monastery for a season. Some go on a series of short-term trips, or intern with a development organization, such as Food for the Hungry. There are, of course, non-Christian opportunities that may be worth considering, Inter Exchange and Go Abroad, for example.

As you make your choice, look for signs of these three stages of initiation: Abandonment, Brokenness, and Dependence.

Be sure to ask questions like these:

ABANDONMENT

- Will the program force me to abandon my comfort zones?

- Will I be gone long enough for abandonment to sink in?

- Will I have a coach who will push me to leave and separate from the people and activities that have defined me at home?

- Will I have a community that will encourage me on my journey?

- Will I be challenged by other cultures and different ways of living?

- Will I receive feedback about what I need to leave?

BROKENNESS

- Does the program encourage brokenness?

- Will I have a coach who will push me to embrace my pain and not give up?

- Will the journey bring me to those with huge needs: the poor, the sick, the oppressed, and the hungry?

- Will I be able to use my brokenness to help others?

- Will I have to surrender my rights and expectations?

- Will it emphasize getting over my needs to serve other people's needs?

DEPENDENCE

- Will I be required to depend on God for food, shelter, or money?

- What basic necessities will I have to struggle for?

- In what ways have past participants seen their faith in God grow?

- How will I be forced to grow in my trust of God?

Kingdom journeys change lives. Jesus used short-term trips to disciple a group of men who turned the world upside down. He continues to use people just like you and me. He first changes our lives. Then he uses us to change others.

Your journey may just be a toe in the water, but if you are to grow, you must go.

Go. It's that simple.

CHAPTER 14: SENDING THEM OUT

"However painful the process of leaving home, for parents and for children, the really frightening thing for both would be the prospect of the child never leaving home." — Robert Neelly Bellah[58]

One of the hardest parts of a kingdom journey is when you're the one staying behind. Parents especially find the experience to be bittersweet. Pushing away from the shore might be thrilling for the one in the boat, but if you're a mom whose life has been devoted to preparing your child to one day leave home on a kingdom journey, the feelings inside can be overwhelming.

Karen and I have run the gamut of emotions as we've sent out each of our four oldest children for a year or more overseas. We have such fun as a family; we laugh, we play games, we tell stories. But when each reached about seventeen years old, we could sense the Gift of Restlessness welling up within them. The familiarity of the home wasn't enough. It was becoming claustrophobic for them.

I remember the first semester of my freshman year in college. The freedom was exhilarating. When Thanksgiving break arrived, it was time to explore the possibilities. How far could you drive from Chicago in a week? With two friends, Dave Wroughton and Dirk Williams, I decided to test the "how far can you drive" theory. We piled into Dirk's Volkswagen Rabbit and headed south. Destination: Acapulco, a mere forty-eight hours away.

First stop on the trip was my parents' house in Missouri. "It's Thanksgiving," they said when we arrived, "Why don't you just stay here?" The thought hadn't even entered my mind. "Thanks, Mom," I said, "but we've got another forty hours to drive before we make it to Acapulco, so we're just going to grab a bite and get going." That's exactly what we did.

Two straight days and nights of driving landed us on the legendary sandy beaches of Mexico's most famous resort. My parents could have tried to stand in our way, but they were wise to let us keep driving. Young people need to experience freedom if they are to grow in wisdom.

Many young people yearn to be set loose to experience life. They want to be trusted. I wrote a blog post encouraging parents to do this and was surprised to see a number of teenagers comment about how restrictive their parents were. A thirteen-year-old wrote, "My dad is worse than any other dad. I'm thirteen, and I still can't go to the park myself. I have freedom, but my parents don't know about it. Like one time I went over to my crazy friend's house and went ding-dong-ditching at midnight."

Young people are going to have to live life for themselves at some point. We parents can help by sending them off with our blessings. The question parents have to answer is, "What will best prepare them to live *their* best lives?"

A kingdom journey can seem extreme to a parent as they consider:

- The risk of a possible mishap while traveling

- The risk of being rejected while sharing our faith

- The risk of not getting along with the team

- The risk of contracting an illness

- The risk of being unprepared to deal with culture shock

Surely there is a less risky way to pass faith on to our children, right? As a parent, I wish there were. The best way I've found is a kingdom journey — a structured form of travel that exposes them to risk, but with some guidance. Society tells us that young people pass into adulthood somewhere between eighteen and twenty-one. Realistically, helping them go on a kingdom journey may be one of the last, best opportunities to impact the direction of their lives.

The world is a dangerous place. Then again, the world has always been filled with risks. Jesus didn't try to soft-sell the risks his disciples would encounter. He didn't leave any small print for them to wonder about. He told them up front that they could expect to be persecuted, handed over to courts, and possibly even killed.

When his disciples appealed to the reasonable requests of family to pull back from the crazy lifestyle, Jesus was brusque, saying, "Who are my mother and brothers?" Even the Son of God knew the importance of leaving home. Before his own journey began, Jesus was baptized and received the blessing of his Father: "This is my Son in whom I am well pleased."

A MOTHER'S FEARS

What's a mother to do? You birth your babies, suckle them,

change their diapers, comfort them, and admonish them as they grow. You see all the things they don't see. You've experienced woundedness and want to save them from such pain. You want them to be happy and you know there are bad people who will take advantage of them. Do you just stop caring? Even if you wanted to, you can't turn off the swirling worries and fears.

I wrote to a mother whose daughter was on a kingdom journey. She let her go despite her misgivings, but she couldn't let her fears go. She lists the things that keep her up at night:

> "I'm afraid she will get sick. I keep warning her to stay hydrated. I think about parasites, bad water, and diseases like malaria or typhoid. I'm afraid she will get in an accident ... the buses get so close to the edge of curvy mountain roads and small, unknown airline companies are prevalent in many countries. The planes are old used ones with mechanical problems. I'm afraid of security issues, that someone will bother her. I guess I've seen too many movies like 'Taken.' I'm afraid of many things.

> "When I don't hear from her in an e-mail, text or a Facebook message, I worry until I hear something... which can be a long time. It's hard not to be irrational and let my imagination run away with scary scenarios. I've had many nights of poor sleep and worry.

> "It's hard to admit that I have a control issue, and it's hard to accept when I am completely

out of control. But on the upside, it forces me to depend on God instead of myself, and causes my faith to grow."

These apprehensions are normal. What's important is that despite one mother's fear, she let her daughter go. It may have been an act of faith, but she let her go, nonetheless.

RISK IS INEVITABLE

One problem is that we live in a risk-averse society and we're sensitized to danger. Our efforts to minimize the risk in our lives are most obviously reflected in our legal system. For several decades, we've all seen a proliferation of lawsuits filed by plaintiffs who complain that they should not be held responsible for a risk they chose to take.

We are also the most insured nation in the world. Consider the array of insurance options which most Americans feel are basic: health, life, disability, liability, automobile, home, and mortgage. All of them attempt to minimize the risk inherent in living.

Of course, some of the best things in life involve great risk. Getting to know someone at a deep level requires being vulnerable with that person. A white-water rafting experience is thrilling because it's risky. Crossing a busy intersection to get to work involves the small risk of being run over.

Then there is the risk that our children will never embrace faith in God as we have. If our job of passing faith on to our kids is a top priority, doesn't it stand to reason that they should experience the reality of it? The substance of our faith is only proved when it is tested. Every day, our society teaches our children to grasp and clutch and satisfy their needs. If society is discipling them to be selfish, what is our response? What are we teaching them? Given that most Christian young people lose their faith after leaving home, we parents need to consider that challenging their faith on a journey is worth all the risks.

RISKS OF NOT GOING

Unfortunately, we can't avoid risk. To do nothing also puts your child in harm's way. What if your child asks to go on a kingdom journey and you discourage him or her out of concern for the risks he or she would face?

Here are a few risks you encounter anyway:

- Your child might inherit a narrow, self-centered worldview.

- Your child might inherit a lukewarm Christianity.

- His or her materialism might never be challenged.

- Your child might live his or her life as taker, not a giver.

In 1976, as a freshman at Wheaton College, I met Ellen Balmer and Phil Tuttle. We went our separate ways after college. They married one another and had two children. This past year I was surprised to learn that their daughter, Emily, was going on a World Race. You always hope that a friend's experience will be all that your own children's experience has been, but that element of risk makes it so unpredictable.

I followed Ellen's blog about her experience as Emily's mom with great interest. Sometimes parents get almost as much out of their child's kingdom journey as their child. I knew my hopes were being realized when Ellen wrote this in the seventh month of the journey:

"I think I'm dehydrated from crying so much. Her blogs are not just telling the stories of broken lives and needy souls; they're revealing her heart... her passion... who she really is.

"But why do they affect me so much? Why do they have to be about so much pain and sadness and brokenness? I have to deal with feelings of conviction, disgust, hatred, anger, helplessness, despair, sadness, and many other unpleasant emotions that rise up in me, as I'm confronted with the harsh reality of the shattered and torn lives of total strangers.

"This is a real dilemma. I've been reading these blogs and they're making me think, they're making me feel, they're making me cry, they're making me wonder... what did I think about or feel before I learned about so many precious but tragic lives?"

Ellen sent Emily off, and she did it well. She couldn't help the fact that her heart was in her throat when Emily traveled. She chose not only to send her, but to go along on the trip emotionally and to experience all that she could with her daughter. You can too.

RELEASING THEM IN STAGES

I was driving down the highway toward Tennessee with our daughter, Estie, who was twenty-two at the time. She was talking about styles of parenting, and how Karen and I have conveyed a sense of responsibility to her and her siblings.

"You guys used a 'phased' approach to launching," Estie

said. "You gave us doses of independence in stages. You encouraged us to save money. When I was thirteen, you made me buy my own clothes. You sent us on mission trips. You helped us to feel competent by giving us miniature experiences prior to launching us."

So all that prepared you to be more independent?" I asked.

"Yes. It not only gave me the chance to not be shocked at leaving home when it was time to go off to school, it also prepared your hearts as parents to release us."

"How does that compare with your friends?" I wondered, truly curious.

"Well, one friend of my friend's has to call home to process every decision she makes. Another friend's mom calls her up every day just to talk. So many parents I'm around talk about their kids' grades or accomplishments way too much. They do it in front of them. It's not healthy."

"But don't you want to encourage your kids?"

"Yeah, but you would give us feedback one-on-one, for example, not in front of people. You didn't stifle our talent and you validated us."

THEY NEED TO LEAVE

Michael Hindes has a good grasp on this issue. He understands that sometimes the best way to love your child is to let them go. Michael and his wife, Kathy, have been married thirty years. They have three sons in their twenties. As a son, Michael experienced the yearning to leave. As a father, he can't deny that his own sons feel the same way. He sees it in their eyes.

As a discipler of young adults, however, Michael also sees

how hard it is for many parents to let them leave. He wrote about the process:

> "It often feels that their walk into destiny is actually a walk away from us. A recurring thought I've had as we raised our sons was that they were trying to move away from us. See, when they crawled, they crawled away. When they walked, they walked away. When they ran, they ran away. We taught them to ride bikes, they peddled away. They got their licenses, they drove away. Now we see them in pursuit of independence and finding their voices. The problem we are having is they are fighting to get independence from us.... It's a painful job this calling to be a parent."

Any parent can relate to the pain of a child who wants to leave. However, this is precisely what we are called to help our children do — leave. None of us wants to stand in the way of our children achieving greatness for the kingdom of God. If we do, we will have a lot to answer for. It's our job to help our kids launch into the destiny God has for them — even if it means we don't catch them every time they fall.

Michael says it well: "Our young adults need places to find their voices and independence. They need places to be exposed to real pain and have the Holy Spirit ask, 'What will you do about it?' They need places with close community that will challenge the behaviors and attitudes that we have previously excused. In short, they need places to grow up and grow away from us."

AN ALTERNATIVE WAY

The alternative to the pattern society gives us is to see our children's leaving as good and necessary. In our basements, they will never learn to provide for themselves. Away from the world's pain, they will never have the opportunity to become someone's hero. Sitting protected from responsibility in coffee shops, their narcissism is a luxury that goes unchallenged. They join a generation that defies the laws of nature where the young gain strength and then totter on the edge of their nests. Falling, they seem headed toward a crash-landing; then they fly away into the wild.

Our culture is the anomaly, not the norm. Our children deserve better. They deserve to be sent. We need to prepare our young people to go. When their time comes, we need to cheer them on, thrilled with the possibilities they will discover once they leave the nest. By all means, give them a grand send-off! Hire a brass band! But let them go.

They have their own stories to write, adventures to live, and heroic deeds to perform. They are part of God's plan to touch and heal the world's pain. Not only is a kingdom journey the spiritual discipline that will bring them fully alive, but it holds the possibility of awakening us, their parents, to new vistas and dreams, as well.

As parents, we must (with Ellen Tuttle) consider the possibility that our own world has grown too small and comfortable. We must consider whether the time has come for role reversal. No longer do we get to lead them, but perhaps they will lead us. What Jesus said about Peter becomes true for us, "When you are old...someone...will lead you where you don't want to go," (John 21:18).

In the book *Culture Shift*, author Albert Mohler, Jr. diagnoses a number of things that are breaking down in our culture. Of particular concern is the poor parenting going on in our homes and families. Today's parents have turned into hyper-protectors, Mohler says. He finds that parents spend a great deal of their time doing little more than protecting their children from life. Mohler says, "Our kids are growing up to be pampered wimps who are incapable of assuming adult responsibility and have no idea how to handle the routine challenges of life."[59]

Parents feel their kids have to excel at everything, even if the parents have to actually do the work. Although error and experimentation are the true mothers of success, parents are taking pains to remove failure from the equation. Smothered by parental attention and decision-making during childhood and adolescence, these young people leave for college without the ability or skill to make their own decisions.

PARENTS SWIMMING UPSTREAM

If you're a parent who sees the issue and is wrestling with what to do, the first step is to get on the same page with your spouse.

Karen and I have a similar philosophy of parenting, so this has been easier for us than many. Yes, it's complicated — too many of us fathers have abdicated our God-given authority role. When we do, who can fault our wives for stepping into the breach and doing what good mothers do best: protect and nurture?

What makes this harder still is that one spouse or the other often knows in their gut that things should be different. Even the best parents are swimming upstream against a lot of junk in our society. Many others have inadvertently engaged in counter-productive behavior, delaying the maturation of their child.

Without realizing it, parents have become chauffeurs and concierges for a generation of children that bounces from Game Boys to soccer practice to Nintendo. In the process comes to assume that life owes them a good time.

Many parents identify so thoroughly with their role that even after their children leave the nest, they are incapable of releasing them to feel the consequences of their own actions. Enmeshed as they are in an identity validated by living vicariously through their children, they helicopter in at various points to rescue their children when they are in peril. For all these reasons, both the child and the parents need a kingdom journey in the worst way. God often uses a child's journey to set crooked things straight in the family.

Deciding to do a kingdom journey can be complicated. Many parents are appropriately attached to their grown children. They have fun together. They're best friends in many respects. But I've seen that even in the best of parent-child relationships, a kingdom journey can complicate the relationship.

No one wants to see their child hurting. And that's why, to a large degree, their child needs to go on the journey. They need to experience pain in the short season. They need to encounter situations that stretch them beyond what they thought they were able to bear. They need to be far away from the familiar sources of comfort. Otherwise, they'll never get to brokenness and from there to dependence.

So how do you sit on the sidelines when it goes against your instincts? Perhaps it's easier for fathers.

Matt is the father of a twenty-something daughter who went on a kingdom journey that lasted a year. Then, a second child went and returned. Matt gives other parents good advice:

"We are but temporary custodians of these children. They have always belonged to God. I miss them when they are gone, and my illusion of power, control and protecting them is stretched really thin. The time and distance is extended, but it was far easier than putting them in a car at sixteen and watching them drive to who-knows-where doing who-knows-what. Prayer is what I held on to then and what I hold on to now."

It's possible for parents to encourage their kids and send them off well. Both parents can find the appropriate balance in letting them go.

Susan, a mom whose daughter took a long kingdom journey said,

"Who am I to stand in the way of my adult child fulfilling the call of the Lord? I would be more afraid of standing in her way than of letting her go. Yes, there are dangers on the trip. But, raising a child, attending a college, going to work, or driving down any street in America is not without risk. I chose to send her with my full blessing."

Psychologists have a term for this stage in a child's maturation process: "individuation." Children appropriately separate from their parents and establish their own identity and beliefs. It requires some space — and yes — some risk.

One of the best things parents can do for their children on a kingdom journey is to pray for them diligently and allow the God and the journey to do accomplish the work.

First, however, parents must allow their children to go — with God.

CHAPTER 14 NOTES

58. Quoted in BrainyQuote.com, *Robert Neelly Bellah Quotes*, http://www.brainyquote.com/quotes/authors/r/robert_neelly_bellah.html.

59. Albert Mohler, Culture Shift: Engaging Current Issues with Timeless Truth, (Colorado Springs, CO: WaterBrook Multnomah Publishers, 2008), 70.

CHAPTER 15: THE END OF RESTLESSNESS

"Good-bye. I am leaving because I am bored." — Last words of author and actor, George Saunders[60]

Jessi Marquez was home. She had traveled to New Zealand and Australia, Thailand and Cambodia, Romania and Ukraine. In Kenya, she was robbed at gunpoint. In Uganda, a friend almost died of malaria. You'd think she would have been overjoyed to return home, but once she had made it back to New York, she felt anything but relief. She was just as uncomfortable as she had been traveling the world.

To celebrate Jessi's return, her friends took her out on the town. Before dinner, she went to one of her best friend's apartment to catch up on her year. Being around Tina was culture shock. She spent an hour talking about all the guys she was dating. She didn't ask about the ministry Jessi did among the hippies in Australia. She didn't ask to hear stories about the orphaned children Jessi fed and held. Tina didn't even ask Jessi about her trip at all. Instead, she asked what she was going to do now that she was home. Jessi replied that she was looking for a job with a church.

"Why?" said Tina. "There's no money in that, no future."

"I'm not really living for that," Jessi said.

Tina's expression showed her confusion, but she didn't say anything. So Jessi asked Tina, "How are you? Are you happy?"

"Of course!" Tina replied. "I have the apartment, the job. Now all I need is the boyfriend!"

"Well, what kind of guy are you looking for?" asked Jessi.

"He definitely has to be cute," stated Tina. "And rich."

"I literally stood in awe," says Jessi. "I didn't know what to say."

Later, when Jessi asked if she would be interested in going to church with her, Tina said that she already had a church she went to — on Christmas and Easter.

"On the way to the restaurant, our cab was stuck in traffic, and we sat in silence. It was so awkward. This was someone I used to be such good friends with, and I just had nothing to say."

Jessi spent the next two days with her city friends. They ate dinner at an exclusive *tapas* restaurant where the bill was $2,000 for their group. They left half their food uneaten. Rather than enjoying the dinner, Jessi thought about how much $2,000 could do in the Philippines, and how many Romanian orphans she could feed with their discarded food.

Jessi wore a simple tank top and jeans to dinner — from the backpack filled with all the clothes she had taken on her kingdom journey, the ones that had mildewed after weeks without washing in Asia and Eastern Europe — while Tina and her friends sported several-hundred-dollar designer dresses. Jessi couldn't bear to pick an outfit from her closet, because it reminded her too much of her past.

Before her kingdom journey, Jessi dressed to impress, choosing outfits based on the tastes of the particular social circle she was with at the time. She had spent her kingdom journey learning what clothes she liked to wear and felt comfortable in.

Jessi once again felt an intense pressure to conform. Amidst her old friends and old lifestyle, doubts began to resurface. Should she have chosen a different outfit? She had been a chameleon in her former life. Should she become one again?

Almost everyone who comes back from a kingdom journey finds life incredibly uncomfortable at some point. You get used to a transient lifestyle. Perhaps your new normal is going out in Mozambique to tell people about God's kingdom or holding Swazi orphans or building camps in Bulgaria or ministering to prostitutes in Cambodia.

You have been transformed. God reveals your true self. You begin walking in that identity: the person God made you to be. Then, you return home and are completely thrown off-kilter.

Normally, people returning from a kingdom journey respond in one of three ways:

1. They backslide, letting the expectations of others lead them back to their old life.

2. They choose to get angry with the people who don't understand what it was like for them on their kingdom journey.

3. Or, they find freedom, learning to be their true self in

the "real" world.

From the moment she returned, Jessi struggled with which path to follow. She wanted to stay on the path of freedom, but she felt like people were trying to drag her back to a life of compromise.

FREEDOM

If kingdom journey gets us to a place where we are free, we've got to be intentional about continuing to walk in freedom after returning home. Jessi had been enslaved by Manhattan's socialite culture with its two standards of excellence — how you look and who you know. A journey broke her free.

Claud was pressured by expectations that he would go to college and take over the family business. Marlena dreamed of the white picket fence American dream, with its good jobs, decent income, and a family. Tiffany had been held hostage by her lifestyle that was good, but ultimately unsatisfying. Nicole was enslaved to her Q-tips and brow powder — the makeup that allowed her to feel beautiful. They had to abandon it all and allow themselves to be broken. They had to become empty before they could experience freedom.

God wants us to be free from judgment, free from comparison, free from our own narcissism, and even free to fail. We go on a kingdom journey to be emptied of all the stuff that gets in the way of this freedom. We leave home knowing that it will change us, but not really knowing what that change will cost. When the breaking that brings change occurs, we experience what the Bible calls the "renewing of our mind."

In other words, we go on kingdom journey to die to ourselves. If we empty ourselves, God can fill us up. If we die, God raises our true self from the dead. If we allow God the freedom to break us, we are set wonderfully free.

Jessi had to go to Malaysia and Uganda. Claud had to go to the slums of Philadelphia and Swaziland. Andrew had to go to Texas. Seth, Jr. had to go to the Philippines. Joe had to go to Budapest. Each traveler learned that the physical freedom of the road is connected to the spiritual freedom of the soul.

A JOURNEY IS NOT ENOUGH

There are limits to what travel alone can accomplish. Journeys need a kingdom focus to move us through the stages of brokenness and into dependence.

In 1909, Ernest Shackleton returned home from his Nimrod expedition to the South Pole to fame and public honor. He was knighted by King Edward and made a Commander of the Royal Victorian Order. He received the Gold Medal of the Royal Geographic Society, and all his crew received a Silver Polar Medal. However, the expedition left Shackleton so heavily in debt that the government had to bail him out with a grant. Even that was not enough to cover the cost of the whole expedition.

To pay off the rest and support his family, Shackleton began a public speaking schedule. He also started several ill-fated business ventures. Each of them failed, leaving him on the edge of poverty. Far from curing the Curse of Restlessness, his journey exacerbated it.

A few years after the expedition, he wrote to his wife, "I am never again going south and I have thought it all out and my place is at home now." But, his public speaking schedule meant that he traveled constantly and was rarely home. With his business ventures failing, he couldn't pay his bills, and despite promises to his wife, his mind drifted to what was left unexplored.

In 1914, five years after returning from Antarctica, Shackleton departed on his infamous Endurance expedition. His ship sunk after striking ice. His crew was hundreds of miles from land with just a few lifeboats. Survival seemed impossible, yet he managed to lead all of his crew of twenty-two to safety. It took three years, but he returned to England.

His Endurance expedition still didn't free him of the Curse of Restlessness. In 1917, he volunteered for the English army to fight in World War I. He returned home, having seen no combat. Once a vehement enemy of all drinking, he became an alcoholic.

In 1920, he began planning another expedition, this time to circle Antarctica and map the continent. A year later, he set off, but did not live long enough to see England again. Despite his heroism at sea, he left his family in shambles. [61]

Shackleton thought he would find freedom on the sea, but he only found alcoholism, loneliness, and death. Richard Rohr calls this the "geographical solution," and says, "We forget we take the old self to the new place."[62] Our surroundings do not change us. We can only have freedom if we allow ourselves to experience brokenness and to move from there to dependence.

Praying, fasting, meditating, and all the other spiritual disciplines won't transform you automatically, either. Just look at some of the very religious Muslims, Hindus, and Christians who live violent and bitter lives. Kingdom journey won't do the work for you; it just brings up the issues that stand between you and intimacy with God — issues that most of us are skilled at avoiding at home.

Kingdom journey also teaches us about God's provision for his children. We don't have to worry about our needs being met. God wants to bless us extravagantly as we depend on him. Rather than having an attitude of scarcity, we can be generous because we know there is so much more than enough.

KINGDOM JOURNEYS AND YOUR LIFE'S FRUIT

It was a sweltering day in the summer of 1959, just before the rainy season when M.A. Thomas began his first kingdom journey. He began out of necessity as much as a desire to depend on God. His journey laid the foundation for a lifelong partnership with God.

Thomas later started a mission organization that planted 43,000 churches among the least reached people in India. He built hundreds of elementary schools, started a Bible institute that has tens of thousands of graduates, and built orphanages that have cared for thousands of children. Thomas said his kingdom journey revealed to him that he should attempt even greater things for the kingdom. So, he did.

Thomas' achievements later in life — the thousands of churches he planted, the hundreds of orphans he helped take care of, the children he helped educate, and the pastors he helped train — all began with his kingdom journey. His kingdom journey was the foundation of his future ministry. After learning radical dependence on God, anything was possible.[63]

CALLING

You have a purpose in life, a vocation, a calling that God wants you to step into. Going on a kingdom journey helps you get to the point where you can begin to understand your call.

In 2008, Andrew Maas was sitting on his couch, eating granola and watching television. It had been several years since his bike trip full of miracles to Texas, and in the meantime he had been on more journeys. He had traveled to Vietnam, Cambodia, Africa, Mozambique, Mexico, and Guatemala — more than a dozen different countries to do missions work, preach the gospel, take care of orphans, and build churches.

Now, back at home, he opened up his laptop, checked his e-mail, and navigated to the blogs of a few friends who were out on their own kingdom journeys. Reading stories of miracles and how people's lives were being changed on their journeys was almost painful. He felt that familiar restlessness. Instead of sitting on a couch in a Colorado suburb, should he be out there on another journey? As Andrew reflected, he found peace — knowing he was where he was supposed to be.

THE NEXT SEASON OF LIFE

On his various journeys, Andrew had ample practice *abandoning* the normal life. He had moved deeply into *brokenness* and *dependence*. Andrew processed his kingdom journeys and continued to grow after returning home. You see, abandonment, brokenness, and dependence are habits we form that lead to three more stages in a life with God: Empowerment, Call, and Confirmation.

If people go on a kingdom journey and do not continue to be discipled, they will be left stranded in the middle of the process and tend to revert to their former selves.

Empowerment is God's strength made perfect in our weakness. Our first and greatest source of empowerment is knowing God's love and provision. When Jesus went through the spiritual gauntlet of temptation with the devil during his forty-day kingdom journey in the wilderness, he found himself tested concerning who he was and what God had promised. He held firmly to the Father's affirmation: "This is my Son, whom I love; with him, I am well pleased" (Matthew 3:17). How marvelous to know that God loves you, no matter what.

Empowerment takes on many forms. Jesus began empowering the disciples, but the Holy Spirit came upon them much later, after an extensive season of prayer. That's when the missions movement began that turned the world upside down.

CONNECTING WITH YOUR PURPOSE

Calling has to do with your purpose — the dream God put in your heart, the vocation you feel you were crafted to pursue.

Frederick Buechner says this about vocation:

> "It comes from the Latin 'vocare,' to call, and means the work a man is called to by God. There are all different kinds of work. The problem is learning which is the voice of God rather than Society, say, or the Super-ego, or Self-Interest.
>
> "By and large a good rule for finding out is this. The kind of work God usually calls you to is the kind of work (a) that you need most to do and (b) that the world most needs to have done. If you really get a kick out of the work, you've presumably met requirement (a), but

KINGDOM JOURNEYS: REDISCOVERING THE LOST SPIRITUAL DISCIPLINE

if your work is writing television deodorant commercials, the chances are you've missed requirement (b).

"Neither the hair shirt nor the soft berth will do. The place God calls you to is the place where your deep gladness and the world's deep hunger meet." [64]

Jennifer Smith went through a horrific phase of her life where she was a homeless addict. After giving her life to Christ and going on a kingdom journey, she felt a calling to minister to the addicts and homeless still on the streets in her hometown. They know that she's been where they are and they love her for it — her ministry is powerful and her calling is sure.

Jesus' example was to press into pain. When he saw the teeming masses of Jerusalem, he felt compassion and sent his disciples to meet their needs. When people showed up asking for healing, he responded by touching them at the point of their pain.

His model is ours to follow. In this world, we'll encounter pain every day if we'll just look for it. I've been blessed with a lot of friends, some of them tremendously successful, but not one of them is without pain. Many have had to struggle with cancer, bankruptcy, broken relationships, and disappointments of all kinds.

They need a touch — they need to know that God cares. If we will allow their pain to touch our hearts, that intersection of love and pain produces something precious — a calling from God.

It's a great thing to feel like God is calling you to something.

Isn't that what you yearn for? Yet, too many people wander through life without a real sense of calling. I believe they need more experience with pain. They need more experience responding to pain with love. Look at anybody you admire — from Mother Teresa to Nelson Mandela — and you'll find that their life was filled with great pain. You'll also see that they met the deep challenge of that pain with love. In so doing, they found the call that defined their lives.

The final stage in what turns out to be a six-stage process is Confirmation. Confirmation comes when your calling is acknowledged by the fruit you bear and by your community. Your contribution brings life to the people around you and they can sense the difference. You become a kingdom builder, a servant leader and the journey continues.

Because a journey inevitably entails risk, you need encouragement all along the way. You need people you respect, people who confirm that you're on the right path and that it's a good thing. We need a community of optimists, friends, spiritual fathers and mothers who when asked, "Is it a good idea to leave on this journey?" can offer the confirmation of a sacred yes. This is a yes to possibility, yes to a version of reality that seems idealistic, impossible even. Young people already dream; they need little help doing this.

But the dream squashers and dream snatchers lay in wait all along life's path. What young people need is someone to help put their wet blanket advice in perspective.

The only reliable resource to confirm one's call is someone who has an objective understanding of all facts — somebody who has the chance to observe us and encourage us. And that's why Jesus put his disciples into a team as they traveled. We need traveling companions.

What a privileged responsibility we spiritual parents have

to help our children run with their dreams. We cheer them on so well when they're on the football field or in the classroom. What about the field of life? Dreams are being birthed and molded in them even now. We should rush to defend that birthing process.

We fathers need to give the sacred yes to chasing after the dream of God for those who have already gone on a journey. The time to protect, to say no, has come and gone — what they need next is encouragement. As my children are entering adulthood, I want them to see and hear me cheering wildly as they learn to dream God-given dreams and then to become stewards of those dreams.

One of the most significant forms of confirmation comes through older and wiser counselors or coaches. A teacher may lay out the facts and the principles, a trainer may spell out the procedures, but it all comes together as life change when a coach watches you and helps you acquire a given skill. A coach observes you, analyzes what you do well or where you need to improve, and then helps you make adjustments. Without a coach you can go for years with a bad habit and never see how it handicaps you. We need their advice. They can see if what we feel called to fits us.

GOD IS WHISPERING

This makes sense, doesn't it? God is whispering in our ears about our greatness in him. It seems impossible. We know all too well our limitations, but God did not make us to be paupers. He made us to be heirs of his kingdom. We are more than conquerors!

When we heed the truth about our greatness in him — when we first hear his whispering voice — the Gift of Restlessness stirs in our souls. We sense God calling us to something more, and it resonates inside of us. The Gift of Restlessness is just a manifestation of our deepest purpose. When we start to step into that greatness and walk in our calling, we find what we sought. Or maybe it finds us. In other words, obedience defeats restlessness.

During the last year of his long stretch of kingdom journeying, Andrew was in Nsoko, Swaziland. He and his team developed sustainable care points to provide for the huge orphan population. The vision was to build locally funded care points that would feed between twenty-five and a hundred orphans a day. Andrew worked to help make businesses more profitable, so that the orphans would be fed through the sponsorship of prospering businesses.

One of their contacts owned a plot of land devastated by a continued drought. If irrigated, the land could employ eight people to farm it; however, the lack of water made it unprofitable. In 2004, well-meaning volunteers raised money for an elaborate pump system. They followed through and gave their time to install it. Unfortunately, when Andrew arrived in 2007, the pump was inoperable — one part of the system had failed. The pumps had been lying there unused for three years lacking one piece of the puzzle. Andrew replaced the missing piece and the farm was soon up and running.

Andrew learned how to advance the Gospel and help businesses profit in poor countries. "A lot of these people wanted to work," he said, "but they needed the resources to be able to start their projects." Andrew's extensive travels opened his eyes to the immense need for business development with a kingdom edge. God was working in his heart, revealing his call.

The Curse of Restlessness that can lead from one trip to the next, one job to the next, or one relationship to the next, can be transformed by a sense of contentment. An abiding peace can grow — a peace that comes from living your calling in the world.

When he returned to the U.S., Andrew completed his business degree by writing a business plan on a micro-finance enterprise in Africa. He even settled down enough to get married. Andrew's calling completed the process that restlessness had started.

This is the long-term goal of kingdom journey: to bring you to a place where you know your identity and role in the kingdom of God, to grow and mature in Christ over a lifetime.

Some might say, "Bloom where you're planted." We say: "Be wrecked for the ordinary."

CONCLUSION: THE BATTLE IS THE LORD'S

Jesus did not content himself with a pastoral ministry in his hometown of Galilee. His heart pounded for the lost. His call was to rescue the oppressed and heal the sick, so he went in search of them. He found them wherever he went — the lame, blind and hungry, all of them pleading for mercy and hope. It ripped at his heartstrings.

Jesus himself, however, touched relatively few people in his lifetime. His mission, instead, was to reach the world through the disciples he was training. They, in turn, would pass the mission on to succeeding generations until his message covered the face of the earth, reaching all nations. Jesus' call to this mission rings forth even today, challenging men and women to serve in his kingdom and to die to themselves.

THE GIFT OF RESTLESSNESS STIRS IN OUR SOULS. WE SENSE GOD CALLING US TO SOMETHING MORE

This is our model in setting out on a kingdom journey — we go to where the poor, oppressed, and hungry live and we discover the kingdom there.

When we go in search of the kingdom of God, we will meet spiritual resistance. We can't escape the reality that there is a battle raging around us. We may struggle like Christ's original followers did to understand how or where to engage, but the battle is the Lord's and we will be victorious in his strength.

Millions are trapped. They live in prisons of hopelessness and despair. Our mission, if we choose to accept it, is to liberate them:

> "He has anointed me to preach good news to the poor. He has sent me to proclaim freedom for the prisoners and recovery of sight for the blind, to release the oppressed, to proclaim the year of the Lord's favor," said Jesus (Luke 4:18-19).

Kingdom journey, Jesus' journey, teaches us to walk in the freedom he has offered. The offer on the table, should we choose to accept it, is to join him on his quest. Kingdom journey is the training grounds for our lifelong partnership with God in setting the captives — and ourselves — free.

CAN YOU DIE HAPPY?

All kingdom journeys have an end, as do all journeys in life. Ultimately, we will have to ask ourselves if we are satisfied with how we've lived. Did we invest our life the way we or God wanted? Did we live well?

My father raised me as a backpacker. We regularly set out,

trudging the trail away from civilization, but at some point we had to turn around and come home. Any journey is that way. The kingdom journeys we take reflect, in part, our great journey through life.

In the end, a kingdom journey is about living our lifelong journey more fully alive. We focus on our relationship with God in the sacred time-space of kingdom journey — so that our longer, more unfocused lifelong journey may be revealed as sacred as well.

To end well, we have to fight our natural tendency toward self-preservation and control. Jesus tells us that losing our life is the only way to discover it. When you give, you receive. When you die, you live. Embracing the reality of our eventual death not only gives context to our loss and suffering, but also frees us to truly live with the time that remains.

It's legend that St. Francis' last words were, "I have done what was mine to do, now you must do what is yours to do."

My friend and mentor Andrew Shearman loves to ask the question, "Can you die happy?" In other words, can you finish your lifelong journey without regrets, having done all that was yours to do?

The question contains a paradox. Death is something most people dread. Funerals are generally dreary affairs. The notion that one can "die happy" runs against the cultural grain. How does a person actually do that?

Dying happy has to do with more than knowing that you're going to heaven; it has to do with fulfilling your purpose on earth. Too many of us allow circumstances and societal expectations to dictate our life's path. We run from the very risks that have the potential to liberate us… to find and fulfill our purpose in life.

Long ago, I made my peace with death and determined to go for broke. Along the way, I've failed, but I have experienced a range of joy and fulfillment that I never would have if I'd chosen a safe life. I think God loves it.

You may have legitimate reasons for not pursuing your dreams. But your life is too precious to make excuses. Maybe old tapes play in your head that say: "You'll never amount to anything." Maybe when you have risked, you have been hurt. Maybe your adventures have ended in shambles. Whatever they are, maybe at long last it's time to get up and get out there again. If you've been attending pity parties, it's time to decline the next invitation.

Perhaps this is the day to say goodbye to the safe life. You don't serve anyone by hiding your best self. God may well be asking you to venture out — to get out on life's stage and go for it. Why not ask God to take you on a kingdom journey and show you how to live fully alive?

Matthew 24:14 speaks of God's dream — his ultimate intent for the world: "This gospel of the kingdom will be preached in the whole world."

My dream is to fill the nations with God's glory and to preach the good news of his kingdom to the ends of the earth.

I love the dream of raising up a generation of people who are fully alive. I'm encouraged as I'm starting to see glimpses that the dream could one day become a reality, especially as more and more disciples begin to embrace their own kingdom journey.

NEW VISTAS IN LIFE

If you are feeling called to kingdom journey, embrace it. The initial thrill of adventure will snap you awake, but eventually will wear off. When you arrive at a place of brokenness, prepare to respond with gratitude to the pain.

Get ready in advance to recognize the emptying process when it comes. It will lead you to the place of dependence — and from there to greater intimacy with God.

Be prepared to practice the secret of being content in whatever circumstance, whether in abundance or in poverty. If you're on kingdom journey right now, lean into the discomfort. God will use it to set you free.

On a kingdom journey, you walk down the path of abandon, you traverse the desert of brokenness, and you rest in the cool shade of dependence. I know — I've been there and will be there again. But the journey is not the destination. You can't stay there. You must descend from the mountaintops and return to the valleys and trenches of imperfect, everyday life.

Journeys with God create a new you... living in a new kingdom. Nothing can be the same again. But, you won't want it to be.

One day — somewhere during or following your own personal journey — you will look out to see incredible vistas of kingdom reality. Freed from your own self-absorption, you will join God in dreaming about his kingdom coming to earth.

No longer a slave to yourself or the world around you, you will see God's purpose and plan for your life.

You will know why you exist. You will know why God created you. Most importantly, you will know how God wants to turn the world upside down through you.

You will also know that he can do it because you've seen it while journeying the world with him.

CHAPTER 15 NOTES

60. Quoted in The Quotations Page, http://www. thequotationspage.com/quotes/GeorgeSaunders.

61. Wikipedia, http://en.wikipedia.org/wiki/Ernest_ Shackleton.

62. Richard Rohr, *On the Threshold of Transformation: Daily Meditations for Men*, (Chicago: Loyola Press, 2010), 13.

63. M.A. Thomas, "Hopegivers' Founder, Dr. MA Thomas," *Hopegivers International*, http://www. hopegivers.org/About-Us/Founder-Dr.-M.A.-Thomas. htm.

64. Frederick Buechner, *Wishful Thinking: A Theological ABC*, (New York: Harper & Row, 1973), 95.

ACKNOWLEDGEMENTS

My name is on the cover, but no one writes a book without help, and I had a lot of it. First, there are the people who helped write the content of the book that I lived:

Joe Bunting was my writing partner before he was my son-in-law. He has been a huge help in getting this book into your hands. It's taken me four years of writing and thinking and still it needed something more - someone to help me take the manuscript the last leg to completion. And just before marrying my daughter Talia, Joe did that. I'm hoping there will be other collaborations to follow.

Karen, saw me ricochet back from Indonesia for the wedding and has been my traveling companion ever since. She's lived the adventures that are in these pages.

Talia, Seth, Estie, Emily, and Leah started out in the back of bikes, cars, and planes, and have had their own fair share of kingdom journeys. I really began to understand the power of kingdom journey when I saw it transforming their lives.

The people who have helped me along the way are too numerous to list. There is our support team — perhaps 40 of them have hung in there since the beginning. These people saw something in us we didn't see in ourselves. And Connie Means is the one non-family supporter who has backed me since I was 17 years old. There's a special place in heaven for saints like her.

Friends like the Watsons and the Hitchcocks helped us stuff the first Adventures envelopes. Heidi Neulander and Lisa Finney believed in us first and worked in the garage with me. Rob Finney actually built that office and so much else in my life.

Sue Mast, Mary Lou Laird, Ron and Darla Campbell; and Dori Beach, were all at the first staff retreat.

Bill Britton, Clint Bokelman, Scott Borg, and Joe Rogers came along not long thereafter and for some reason, haven't left me yet.

Anna-Marie Franken was originally a partner in Swaziland and then became a partner in the vision of a year-long kingdom journey. God gave her a dream that it could happen and it took a year's mileage in my journey to get my arms around it and see God's point.

Andrew Shearman stirred up my vision for the kingdom and has loved me well.

Gary Black and Tom Davis are brothers who I'm doing the journey of life with.

Michael Hindes took the World Race for four years and helped prove the concepts contained in this book.

Then there are those who helped me specifically on this book project:

Dan Brock transcribed a lot of my writings.

Emily Drevets spent a summer helping me shape the first manuscript.

Ashlie Offenburg helped in the editing process.

Jeff Goins has done a better job of taking my mentoring than anyone else. He has helped me shape the manuscript and get it in your hands.

Robert Sutherland is a master editor. He cleaned up the final draft.

Mark Oestreicher saw the book's potential and has

encouraged me to make sure it finds its audience.

Allie Lousch put the last touches on the final draft at a time when we were all sick of the project.

THANK YOU ALL FOR SPEEDING ME ON MY JOURNEY AND SHAPING THIS MESSAGE IN WAYS THAT I COULD NOT. YOU ARE ALL TANGIBLE EVIDENCE TO ME THAT GOD IS PERSONAL AND CARING.

BIBLIOGRAPHY

Antiphanes. Quoted in BrainyQuote.com. *Antiphanes Quotes.* http://www.brainyquote.com/quotes/authors/a/antiphanes.html.

Augustine, St. *Confessions.* Translated by Henry Chadwick. Oxford, England: Oxford University Press, 2008.

Barna Group. "Research on How God Transforms Lives Reveals a 10-Stop Journey." *Barna Group: Examine. Illuminate. Transform.* http://www.barna.org/transformation-articles/480-research-on-how-god-transforms-lives-reveals-a-10-stop-journey.

Bell, Rob. Quoted in Josh Lujan Loveless. "Is Rob Bell a Universalist." *Relevant: God. Life. Progressive Culture.* http://www.relevantmagazine.com/god/church/features/25030-is-rob-bell-a-universalist.

Bono. Quoted in "Transcript: Bono remarks at the National Prayer Breakfast." *USA Today.* http://www.usatoday.com/news/washington/2006-02-02-bono-transcript_x.htm.

Booth, William. Quoted in ThinkExist.com. *William Booth Quotes.* http://thinkexist.com/quotes/william_booth/.

Brainard, David. Quoted in BrainyQuote.com. *David Brainerd Quotes.* http://www.brainyquote.com/quotes/authors/d/david_brainerd.html.

Branch, Rickey. Quoted in BrainyQuote.com, *Branch Rickey Quotes.* http://www.brainyquote.com/quotes/

authors/b/branch_rickey.html.

Bridges, Jerry and Bob Bevington. *The Bookends of the Christian Life.*Wheaton, IL: Crossway Books, 2009.

Brooks, David. "Social Animal: How the New Sciences of Human Nature can Help Make Sense of Life." *The New Yorker.* http://www.newyorker.com/reporting/2011/01/17/110117fa_fact_brooks.

Buechner, Frederick. *Secrets in the Dark: A Life of Sermons.* New York: HarperCollins, 2006.

Buechner, Frederick. *Wishful Thinking: A Theological ABC.* New York: Harper & Row, 1973.

Chandler, Adam. "For Refugees, a Modern Exodus." *InTheMoment.* http://momentmagazine.wordpress.com/2011/01/06/for-refugees-a-modern-exodus/.

Chesterton, G.K. Quoted in The Quotations Page. http://www.thequotationspage.com/quote/26278.html.

"College Students Have Less Empathy than in Past, Study Shows." *Annals of Psychotherapy & Integrative Health.* http://www.annalsofpsychotherapy.com/articles/news/149/15/College-Students-Have-Less-Empathy-Than-in-Past-Study-Shows.

Collins, Gary R. "Starting Over." *Gary R. Collins,* no. 335. 2009. http://www.garyrcollins.com/newsletter.php?letterid=34.

Descartes, René. *A Discourse on Method: Meditations on the First Philosophy Principles of Philosophy.* Translated by John Veitch. London, England: Orion Publishing Group, 2004.

Dylan, Bob. "Gotta Serve Somebody." *Slow Train*

Coming. New York: Columbia Records, 1979.

"Endurance." Wikipedia, http://en.wikipedia.org/wiki/ Endurance_%281912_ship%29.

Foster, Richard J. *Celebration of Discipline.* New York: HarperCollins Publishers Inc., 1998.

Gide, Andre. Quoted in BrainyQuote.com, *Andre Gide Quotes.* http://www.brainyquote.com/quotes/authors/a/ andre_gide.html.

Hayden, Sterling. *Wanderer.* Dobbs Ferry, New York: Sheridan House, 2000.

Holton, Chuck. "Are Short-Term Mission Trips Effective." *CBN News.* http://www.cbn.com/ cbnnews/569604.aspx.

Kerouac, Jack. *On the Road.* New York: Penguin Books, 1999.

Kierkegaard, Soren. Quoted in Dan Rockwell. "10 Ways to Become a Risk-Taker." *LeadershipFreak. wordpress.com.* http://www.leadershipfreak.wordpress. com/2012/04/10/10-ways-to-become-a-risk-taker.

Krakauer, Jon. *Into the Wild.* New York: Anchor Books, 1997.

Kullberg, Kelly Monroe and Lael Arrington. *A Faith and Culture Devotional: Daily Readings in Art, Science, and Life.* Grand Rapids, MI: Zondervan, 2008.

Layrus, Dan. "Boston." *All the Stars and Boulevards.* New York: Epic Records, 2005.

Lewis, C.S. *The Weight of Glory: And Other Addresses.* New York: HarperCollins Publishers, Inc., 1980.

Maillart, Ella, Quoted in BrainyQuote.com, *Ella Maillart Quotes*, http://www.brainyquote.com/quotes/authors/e/ella_maillart.html.

McDonald, Gordon. "Leader's Insight: So Many Christian Infants," *Leadership Journal*, http://www.christianitytoday.com/le/2007/october-online-only/cln71001.html?start=2.

Menon, Mohan K. and Alex Sharland. "Narcissism, Exploitative Attitudes, and Academic Dishonesty: An Exploratory Investigation of Reality Versus Myth." *Journal of Education for Business*. 86:50-55 (2011), 50-55.

Mitchell, Joni. "Rainy Night House." *Ladies of the Canyon*. Burbank, California: Reprise Records, 1970.

Mohler, Albert. *Culture Shift: Engaging Current Issues with Timeless Truth*.Colorado Springs, CO: WaterBrook Multnomah Publishers, 2008.

Neelly-Bellah, Robert. Quoted in BrainyQuote.com. *Robert Neelly Bellah Quotes*. http://www.brainyquote.com/quotes/authors/r/robert_neelly_bellah.html.

Nouwen, Henri. *Bread for the Journey*. San Francisco: HarperCollins, 1997.

Onoda, Hiroo. *No Surrender: My Thirty-Year War*. Annapolis, MD: Naval Institute Press, 1999.

Orvell, Tamar. "In Tel Aviv: The Orange on the Passover Seder Plate." *Only Connect: A dual citizen's wide-angle lens, dispersing dots of light*. http://www.only-connect.blogspot.com/2009/04/om-tel-aviv-orange-on-passover-seder.html.

Page, Jimmy and Robert Plant. "Stairway to Heaven." *Led Zeppelin IV*. New York: Atlantic, 1971.

Pew Forum on Religion and Public Life, "Religion Among the Millennials," http://www.pewforum.org/Age/Religion-Among-the-Millennials.aspx.

Picasso, Pablo. Thinkexist.com, http://thinkexist.com/quotation/i_am_always_doing_that_which_i_cannot_do-in_order/217965.html.

Potts, Rolf. *Vagabonding: An Uncommon Guide to the Art of Long-Term World Travel.* New York: Villard Books, 2002.

Rohr, Richard *Adam's Return: The Five Promises of Male Initiation.* New York: Crossroad Publishing Company, 2004.

Rohr, Richard. *On the Threshold of Transformation: Daily Meditations for Men.* Chicago: Loyola Press, 2010.

Saunders, George. Quoted in The Quotations Page. http://www.thequotationspage.com/quotes/GeorgeSaunders.

Shackleton, Ernest. Wikipedia, http://en.wikipedia.org/wiki/Ernest_Shackleton.

Shedd, John A. "Salt from my Attic," in *The Yale Book of Quotations 2006,* Edited by Fred R. Shapiro. New Haven, CT: Yale University Press, 2006.

Shellenbarger, Sue ."Delaying College to Fill in the Gaps." *Wall Street Journal.* http://online.wsj.com/article/SB10001424052970203513204576047723922275698.html.

Springsteen, Bruce. "Born to Run." *Born to Run.* Los Angeles: CBS Records, 1975.

Stamper, Gary. "Men are Hurting." *The Integral*

Warrior. http://www.garystamper.blogspot.com/2010/05/men-are-hurting.html.

Stipe, Michael. "It's the End of the World as We Know It (And I feel Fine)." Single 45 Record. Hollywood, CA: I.R.S. Records, 1987.

Sweet, Jesse and Daniel Gilbert. *PBS: This Emotional Life.* Television series segment. Boston: WGBH, premiered September 2009.

Thomas, M.A. "Hopegivers' Founder, Dr. MA Thomas." *Hopegivers International.* http://www.hopegivers.org/About-Us/Founder-Dr.-M.A.-Thomas.htm.

Turner, Victor. *The Ritual Process: Structure and Anti-Structure.*Berlin: Aldine De Gruyter, 1969.

Twenge, Jean and W. Keith Campbell. *The Narcissism Epidemic: Living in the Age of Entitlement.* New York: Free Press, 2009.

Walborn, Ron. *Grieving the Seasons of Our Lives.* Podcast Audio. Personal Spiritual Formation, MP3, 50. http://www.adventures.org/podcasts/psf/grievingtheseasonsofourlives.mp3.

ABOUT THE AUTHOR

Seth Barnes is a work in process.

The son of a physician and prayer warrior, he embarked on his first mission trip in high school. During that two-month adventure in Guatemala, Seth was exposed to poverty he never knew existed. It changed him.

Before graduating from Wheaton College, Seth joined a mission to Peru and later worked in a Thai refugee camp for Cambodians fleeing the Khmer Rouge. Soon after graduation, he married Karen, and they left the United States to serve as missionaries in Indonesia and the Dominican Republic. A few years later, he earned his MBA at the Darden School of Business, University of Virginia.

In 1989, Seth began Adventures in Missions in his garage. From that modest beginning, Adventures has equipped and sent over 100,000 missionaries to connect the body of Christ to the needs of a weary world. Through the process, Seth grew to understand the importance of a relationship - and conversation - with God, which has guided his entire ministry and life.

Seth and his wife, Karen, have raised five children in Gainesville, Georgia. You can find him online at sethbarnes.com

CPSIA information can be obtained at www.ICGtesting.com
Printed in the USA
LVOW062311300712

292138LV00001B/14/P